10/26/14

Dear Vladimir and Marilia,

I hope you enjoy
my book. Thank you
very much for all of
your wonderful help!

Best regards,
Susan

101
WAYS
TO BE
YOUR OWN
BEST FRIEND

A Guide to the Art of Fully Living

Susan Bregman, PhD

ISBN: 978-1-4834-0868-2 (sc)
ISBN: 978-1-4834-0867-5 (e)

Library of Congress Control Number: 2014902962

Lulu Publishing Services rev. date: 02/20/2014

DEDICATED WITH LOVE ...

To the memory of Ralph, Mom, Dad and Gil

Contents

Acknowledgements

My deepest personal thanks go to the following people for their encouragement and support: My editor, Marian Sandmaier, whose vision of clarity helped sharpen my writing; my reader, Ralph Dannheisser, for his eagle eye and generous help with editing; Jason Bregman, Brian Bregman and Dr. Marita Danek for their input on content and flow. A special thank you goes to my clients who taught me so much over the years and enriched my life; Virginia Satir who taught me about peace within, peace between and peace among and my wonderful family and friends for their love and support.

Author's Note

In order to protect confidentiality, the names and identifying information in case histories that are reported in this book have been changed. Do not do the exercises in this book if you feel emotionally unstable, or have had a history of psychiatric disorders, without first consulting a qualified mental health professional.

Introduction

My neighbor and I were standing in his garage as he told me about his latest project. He and his wife had bought a big piece of land in Virginia and they were building a home on it. Between his job, family responsibilities and now this new home project, he admitted that he felt "overwhelmed." To me, he looked as though he might burst with anxiety.

"Butch," I said, "do you know how to eat an elephant?"

He looked at me puzzled. "No."

Smiling, I said, "One bite at a time!"

Years later, Butch told that he never forgot that bit of "wisdom" and it helped him through many difficult situations in his life.

This book covers many aspects of daily experience that I hope will be helpful to you—one day (one bite) at a time. You will have the opportunity to learn mental health skill-building techniques—including visualizations and meditations to help with stress reduction; communication skills for enriching relationships; coping with fears; setting goals; dealing with anger; deepening values, beliefs and self-knowledge; graceful aging; expressing your authentic voice through journaling, and mastering self-care approaches. Adopting these techniques can assist you in tapping into your natural capacity for self-compassion and emotional empowerment.

Read just one page per day. If you feel you are not able to truly concentrate and reflect on that page, read it again the next day and even the day after that one. In other words, *take your time.* Do not go on to the next page until you have had a chance to reflect on each topic and think about how it affects your life. If there is a particular topic that you need help with, go to the table of contents to find the day or days that relate to that issue.

Our time here on earth is really quite short, this we know for sure. You arrive here with your self and you continue on the entire journey as your main companion. You are totally unique, with fingerprints to prove it. Cherish that uniqueness and become your own best friend!

"It is not the place we occupy which is important, but the direction in which we move."

—Oliver Wendell Holmes

"It is never too late to be who you might have been."

—George Eliot

Positive Thinking

Whatever you think about, you become. If negative thoughts are constantly running through your brain, your life will move in a negative direction. But if you focus on the positive aspects of your life, it will move in a positive direction.

Describe your day as you normally would. Now describe it as an optimist would.

Notice the difference!

Think about your brain as if it were a computer and your thoughts were the software installed inside it. You want to install healthy thoughts in your computer and keep out viruses. Tune into your thoughts on a regular basis and make sure that you are not doing any "stinkin thinkin." If you catch yourself thinking negative thoughts, change them to positive ones.

"The unexamined life is not worth living."

—Socrates

I was working with a beautiful 35-year-old woman who had experienced severe trauma in childhood. As a child, she had accepted abuse from others, hating and blaming herself. As an adult, when people said nice things to her, she would misinterpret them as negatives because she was still seeing her life through the eyes of the unloved, abused child. With time and consistent work, she was able to leave her past behind and begin to see herself as the lovely person of the present who deserved love and nurturing. She learned how to clear out old negative patterns from her mind and make room for new, positive thoughts. She began to see that she could *choose* her attitude.

The Power of a Positive Mindset

A positive mindset can have a powerful effect on your life and overall sense of well-being. Sometimes small changes in your thinking can make a huge difference. Try this: write a list of 25 positive thoughts. Then, recite aloud one thought each day. You can do this in the morning when you are taking your vitamins or eating breakfast. As you focus on that positive thought, take the time to consider it slowly, and reflect on it during the day.

There is something special about making a daily commitment. This might seem like a small gesture, but one positive thought per day adds up to 365 positive thoughts a year!

"A man is but the product of his thoughts. What he thinks, he becomes."
—Mahatma Gandhi

So often, we focus on the things that go wrong in our lives rather than noticing all of the things that are actually working well. By focusing on what is working, we create a mindset of gratitude.

There are at least two ways to look at each situation: negatively or positively. When you reframe a negative thought into a positive one, what you are actually doing is analyzing the situation carefully and looking for the positive message in it. You will often find one.

Have you ever thought of focusing on the "near misses" in your life? By that, I mean situations that were almost disasters or problems but worked out well. You will be surprised to see how many of them you can remember. For example, I was slowing down to a stop sign in my neighborhood. It was dusk and the visibility was poor. I suddenly noticed a boy on a bike heading right toward my car. Had I not adequately slowed down, I might have hit him. That was a near miss that I am extremely grateful for!

$\mathcal{P}$ositive $\mathcal{P}$sychology

Dr. Martin E.P. Seligman, founder of the field of positive psychology and author of *Learned Optimism* and *Authentic Happiness*, is well known for his fascinating and thorough research on the topic of happiness. Seligman found that for many people, overall happiness was defined by three qualities: flow, meaning and pleasure.

FLOW: This is the experience of total engagement, such as being so involved in listening to music that it feels as though no dividing line exists between yourself and the music. This same experience might occur when you are cooking, watching a movie or sports, playing with a child, walking in the woods or some other activity that stimulates total engagement. The key is to be mindful of discovering things that you love to do. Today might be the day to sign up for that pottery or bicycle repair class!

MEANING: Developing a sense of meaning and purpose in your life, be it small or large, leads to fulfillment and happiness. Volunteer work has that effect on many people. Providing service brings you out of yourself and enhances life's meaning.

PLEASURE: Momentary bodily and mental experiences which enhance delight and provide comfort. Examples are the enjoyment of a massage or the satisfaction of a delicious meal. Grateful thoughts can also heighten pleasurable feelings.

"We act as though comfort and luxury were the chief requirements of life, when all that we need to make us happy is something to be enthusiastic about."

—Charles Kingsley

Reinforce the Good Feelings

"Interests evolve into hobbies or volunteer work which grows into passions. It takes time, more time than anyone imagines."
—Po Bronson

You might not be totally aware of where your passion lies. One good way to find out is to experiment with different hobbies and classes. Trying out new things often takes courage, but once you get into them, you will find it is extremely enriching.

Allow yourself to be open to the positives and actively seek them out. Take the time to keep them in your awareness. For example, when you smell a rose, pause and take in the fragrance. Linger there for an extra moment. When you hug a friend, linger there, too!

When you notice that you are feeling good about a situation, take a few minutes to write about what is happening for you. (Preferably, jot it down in a journal.) Then, read that note once a week to reinforce the positive memory. This will strengthen positive neural pathways in your brain, reinforcing the good feelings. *The Happiness Advantage,* by Shaun Achor, will provide you with more information on this important subject. Several engaging You Tube presentations highlight his work.

Just thinking about someone who is a positive force in your life will stimulate the bonding hormone known as oxytocin. This by itself can put you in an excellent frame of mind. Take the time to send a note, or an e-mail, or make a call to someone you're thinking about. Research has demonstrated that having a strong social network boosts the immune system.

Try and Try Again

I once had a client, Donna, who was unhappy with her overweight body. She had successfully gone through Overeaters Anonymous (OA) five years before, lost weight and felt wonderful. But due to family and work stress, over the next few years Donna had gained back the weight. I encouraged her to go back to OA but she refused. "It didn't work before," she said, "so why would it work this time?"

I responded: "Oh, but it *did* work before! You gained the weight back over several years because of a variety of circumstances. But that doesn't cancel out the fact that you *had* success with the program."

Nonetheless Donna was adamant about not wanting to go back to O.A. Soon after that, she left counseling. Three years later she came back to see me regarding caring for her elderly mother. I noticed that she had lost a lot of weight. She said that the previous year, she had made a decision to go back to O.A—and it made all the difference! She looked and felt terrific, and was starting a new chapter in her life.

Beware of saying that something "just doesn't work." Sometimes you have to go through many trials with something before it takes hold.

"I know God will not give me anything I can't handle. I just wish that He didn't trust me so much."

—Mother Teresa

You Can Train Your Brain

Stay with me here as I talk about your—brain! It might sound a bit complex at first, but it is really rather simple and extremely fascinating. The human brain is flexible and continues to grow and change in response to experiences throughout our lives. We now know that you *can* "teach an old dog new tricks." Experiences, mental activities and interactions with others actually produce changes and growth in the physical structure of the brain.

Billions of neurons, which conduct information, are located in your brain. As you develop new habits, these neural pathways become stronger and more complex. It is like creating a new track on a path. As you continue to walk regularly on the path, the track becomes deeper and deeper.

If there is a new habit that you want to cultivate, pay close attention to developing the neural pathways in your brain for that new habit. Over time, you will have more control over that amazing system, the brain!

For example, let's say that you want to start developing the new habit of meditating for 10 minutes a day. Build your new "meditation neural pathways." Practice meditating every day. Over time, these neural pathways for meditating will grow and become more complex. The habit will become more ingrained within you and the tracks will become deeper. Before long, meditating will be a natural part of your life.

As you gain more control over how your brain functions, you will enjoy a greater sense of running your own life—instead of having it run you!

When you take breaks from your meditation practice, resume as soon as possible. For example, if you go on a vacation, start your practice again as soon as you return home.

For more information on this topic, you might want to explore two excellent books filled with "brain-changing" exercises: *Just One Thing: Developing a Buddha Brain One Simple Practice at a Time,* by Rick Hanson, Ph.D. and *Bouncing Back: Rewiring Your Brain for Maximum Resilience and Well Being,* by Linda Graham, M.F.T.

Use Brain-Training to Develop New Habits

Julie wanted to start walking on a daily basis to enhance her health and well being. Her conflict, however, was that she also wanted to stay in bed and sleep longer. What to do? She decided to change the physical structure of her brain by changing her experiences.

In our work together, we developed a guided imagery. In the imagined scene, she saw her sneakers walking out the door, followed by an image of herself running after them, catching up and jumping into them. As she closed her eyes and imagined that picture, she made it big and bright. She said to herself with enthusiasm: "Walking will help my health and well being; it will give me more energy and keep me feeling stronger and younger." Julie decided to make walking her top priority and told herself that it would be the most important thing that she did every day. She was determined to walk first thing in the morning, so that nothing else got in the way of her commitment.

When she woke up the next morning, Julie began building her new neural pathways for walking. The imagery propelled her to get out of bed and follow through on her plan. (She wanted to catch her sneakers before they ran off without her!) Then, during the day she practiced the imagery. By repeating this on a daily basis, she began to build new, "pro-walking" neural pathways. She strengthened them further by giving herself positive reinforcement—Great job! You're getting stronger!—at the end of her walk.

"Go confidently in the direction of your dreams. Live the life you've imagined."

—Henry David Thoreau

Train Your Brain to Shift Perspective

Feelings are expressed through emotions and bodily sensations. They tend to come and go in your mental world like ocean waves, constantly shifting and changing from turbulent to calm states. For example, if worry is a problem for you, get in the habit of saying to yourself, "I FEEL worried" instead of "I AM worried". This small shift will help you to become aware of the fact that feelings come and go and you don't have to be engulfed by them. You will notice the feelings but not "own" them as if they are yours forever.

By simply observing your thoughts, feelings and behaviors, you can create positive changes in your life. For example, if you are experiencing a lot of anxiety, observe each symptom as just a bodily sensation, thought or emotion. Take a slow, deep breath and say to yourself: "I notice that my stomach is queasy and the muscles in my neck are tight now." Now take another slow, deep breath and say: "I notice that my jaw is tight now." This way of thinking will help you to step outside of yourself and shift perspective. You will begin to see yourself from the outside looking in.

The book *Mindsight,* by Daniel Siegel, MD, provides a useful resource on this topic of stress management through mindfulness.

Noted psychotherapist Virginia Satir suggested that when you notice tightness or discomfort in your body, you give that sensation a message of appreciation for letting you know that it is there. As you notice and acknowledge bodily sensations and emotions, they change and sometimes dissolve. Staying in touch with your breathing will also help you to relax and move beyond uncomfortable physical and emotional states.

"Feelings come and go like clouds in a windy sky. Conscious breathing is my anchor."

—Thich Nhat Hanh

Old Brain / New Brain and Your Emotions

Understanding how your brain functions will provide you with a powerful new lens through which to experience your life.

Your brain has three different kinds of logic. One part of your brain is concerned with physical sensations such as sound, sight, smell, taste and touch. It moves you towards pleasure and away from pain. This is an old part of your brain known as the reptilian brain.

Another part of your brain is known as the limbic brain, a part run by the amygdala. It is concerned with your safety and survival and it is a throwback to the days when your ancestors were cave dwellers fearing for their lives. In times of danger the choices are fight, flight or freeze.

The new brain is concerned with problem solving, making choices and gaining knowledge. This neurological "thinking cap" is known as the cognitive brain.

When you are upset, worried or angry, the old brain steps in and gets ready to either fight back or run away from the real or perceived danger. It dominates the thinking cap, because during those cave days, action was the first line of defense. Survival often depended on the quick activation of the old brain.

It is important to understand that the old brain operates with little intelligence and just pure reaction. In order to calm it down, you need to take a deep breath and slowly count to ten. Now, give yourself a moment to pause and allow your thinking cap a chance to wake up, step in and help you think logically about what to do next. You will then be able to loosen the grip of fear, enter a calm, more accepting state of mind and take stock of the situation with your thinking cap. The more you are aware of this brain-shifting process, the more power you will have to change the way you react in difficult situations.

Meditation: The Practice

Meditation has been around for thousands of years and has proven to be an extremely effective tool for the development of emotional well-being. The best way to get into the habit of meditating is to do it on a regular basis even for only five minutes a day. A small, regular commitment will bring success.

The key to effective meditation is to observe thoughts passing through your mind but not pay close attention to them. While this skill takes many years for most people to fully achieve, it is extremely helpful even in the beginning stages of practice. As you meditate, you learn what it feels like to live fully in the present moment. You start to understand the solid and unchanging nature of your true essence.

When your mind starts to wander, bring it back by focusing on your breathing. New neural networks will develop through practice and, in time, meditation will become easier and more natural. Don't be discouraged if you find yourself repeatedly coming back to your thoughts. Everyone does this. People often think that they are not capable of meditating because their mind is constantly racing from one thought to another.

But this is not true. In fact, when your mind is active, it provides you with the opportunity to practice regulating it, and strengthening your willpower. When you are able to settle your mind for only a minute—or even a few seconds, at first—that is genuine progress.

Observe that between each thought there is a small gap. Imagine yourself expanding that gap and stretching it out just a little. This will provide you with more opportunity to quiet your thoughts. Also notice as you breathe, there are gaps between breaths. Focusing on those gaps will slow down your breathing as well.

By bringing your mind back to the moment, you also become aware that you *are* in charge of your mind. Through regular mediation, you will make better choices, develop more compassion towards others, improve your sleep, and experience a stronger sense of emotional balance. This is because meditation helps you to develop a settled feeling from within the depths of your being, which will enhance your perspective and your relationships.

Because you are changing your relationship with your thoughts and paying more attention to yourself, you are also providing the potential for increased self-esteem—just one more powerful benefit of your practice.

Meditation: The Power of the Present Moment

For most of his early life, Ekhart Tolle experienced frequent episodes of anxiety and suicidal depression. He felt that his life was without meaning. When he was 29 years old, he made a decision to end his life. As he contemplated suicide, a strange awareness overcame him. If he didn't want to live with himself, one person was "he" and another person was "himself." Did that mean that there were two of him, one who hated him and one who listened?

As a result of that awareness, he came to realize that he was more than a bundle of self-critical thoughts. He started to notice the other part of him, which was not his ego-self but something much larger. This new awareness set Ekhart on a path of spirituality and a renewed desire to live.

Over time, he came to write *The Power of Now*, which became a best-selling book on spiritual enlightenment. This book has helped thousands of people understand their journey from the analytical mind to the conscious mind—a journey towards enlightenment. His words are simple and yet extremely powerful. He believes that as you begin to trust your body, it will provide messages about how you feel and what you need.

One meditation technique that incorporates this body awareness is called the "arm lift." It helps to put you in a relaxed, open state and prepares you for further meditation.

You may want to try it and see if it is a good "fit" for you.

Close your eyes, get in touch with your breathing, and be present in this moment. Slowly lift your right arm straight out in front of you. Notice that you know where your arm is without seeing it. Move your arm slowly to the right and keep focusing on it with your mind's eye. Now move your arm over to the left and allow yourself to fully experience what these movements are like for you. Move it back to the center. Now, move it slowly up and down and slowly wave it, side to side, in the air. Now let it fall gently into your lap again.

Continue to be in touch with your breathing and when you are ready, open your eyes. Notice how relaxing it feels just to do this simple exercise. Now do a few moments of gentle breathing and allow your thoughts to float away.

Meditation: The Peaceful Heart

According to the HeartMath Research Institute in Santa Cruz, California, breathing in positive emotions while focusing on your heart actually steadies your heart rate.

Take five minutes out of your day to do this exercise. Find a comfortable seat. Close your eyes, go inside yourself and focus on your breathing. Take six slow, deep breaths. Place your hand on your heart and feel the warmth radiating from your hand. Breathe into your heart center, slowly and deeply. Think of peace, calmness and safety. Stay in touch with your breathing and think of contentment, well-being, kindness for yourself and gratitude for others. Take ten slow deep breaths while continuing to keep your hand on your heart. Now, slowly and gently open your eyes.

Here is another exercise related to the heart. Breathe into your "heart center." While placing your hand on your heart, recall moments in your life when you felt safe and loved. Bring to mind someone who loves you unconditionally. Studies have shown that these loving thoughts alone can release oxytocin, which is known to promote trust and bonding.

Merely placing your hand on your heart and feeling the warm touch of your own hand releases the hormone as well. These activities are so simple yet have such a powerful impact!

The Heartmath Solution, by Doc Childre and Howard Martin, provides fascinating information on the understanding and use of the heart's energy.

"Nothing can bring you peace but yourself."
—Ralph Waldo Emerson

DAY 13

Meditation: Mindfulness

Each day, take a few minutes to think of something that you are grateful for. This process is known as "practicing gratitudes." It will help you to experience more positive emotions on a day-to-day basis. You will find numerous books and articles about how the practice of daily gratitudes lowers blood pressure, boosts the immune system and increases longevity. That is how powerful our thoughts are. Dr. Cristiane Northrup, author of *Women's Bodies, Women's Wisdom* describes this concept as "A thank-you a day can keep sickness away."

Your body can't tell the difference between anxiety and excitement. It produces the same energy lift. So, when you have an event, such as a party or an important meeting coming up and you are feeling "anxious," ask yourself if you are actually anxious or excited. This is a subtle difference but an important one. You may find that excitement is what you're really feeling. Then go for it!

When you are feeling anxious your mind constricts; it is as though you are looking at the sky through a pipe. A good meditation is to remove the pipe in your mind's eye and see the entire sky! Now, breathe.

Add this to your mindfulness practice:

"Throughout the day, take breaks to walk mindfully at a very slow pace. It is very refreshing and calming, even when done for about five minutes."

—Charlette Mikulka

When Mikulka speaks of "mindfully," she means clearing your mind and focusing on the present moment as you walk. Her book *Peace in the Heart and Home* provides a wealth of information on psychological well-being.

Overcome Your Fear and Just Do It!

When you are afraid to try something new, and find yourself making excuses as to why you "can't," try pushing yourself anyway. Make a decision to challenge your fear. This will be the start of a much more satisfying life.

"The task we must set for ourselves is not to feel secure, but to be able to tolerate insecurity".

—Eric Fromm

When confronted with a fearful situation, the emotional part of the brain quickly shifts to a fight-or-flight mode, activating a rapid heartbeat, tight stomach and many other physical symptoms. While these can be scary feelings, they are not dangerous and they will pass. If you jump ahead and "just do it," in time you will feel your body calming down and your confidence increasing.

Some excellent books on the subject are: *Feel the Fear and Do it Anyway* by Susan Jeffers, *Triumph over Fear* by Jerilyn Ross and *Courage is a Three Letter Word—Yes* by Walter Anderson.

"I've been absolutely terrified every moment of my life—and I've never let it keep me from doing a single thing I wanted to do."

—Georgia O'Keefe

If you are familiar with O'Keefe's unique and controversial paintings, you will truly appreciate this quote.

DAY 15

The Pause

Dr. Ilana Rubenfeld, author of *The Listening Hand: Self-Healing Through the Rubenfeld Synergy Method of Talk and Touch,* was a symphony conductor in New York who turned to body work to heal muscle spasms that were paralyzing her arms. As a result of this personal work she eventually developed the Rubenfeld Synergy Method, which combines touch and psychotherapy. Ilana once asked her seminar participants: "What is the most important element in music, without which music would not exist?"

The answer is "the pause." The pause is absolutely necessary in order to create music. You need pauses in your life to create balance, peace and harmony. If you are living a full, active life, you may forget to pause now and then. But pausing is vital—in music and in life.

It is especially important to pause before you act out impulsively. Think about it before pushing the "send" button on that emotionally laden e-mail that you just prepared. Take three deep breaths, and then give yourself a chance to think about what you want to accomplish before you do something that you might regret later.

Remember that whenever you feel threatened, the old brain kicks into a fight-or-flight position, readying itself to help you survive and keep you safe. By pausing, you give the newer thinking part of your brain a chance to assert itself, analyze the situation and think through a much better solution to the issue at hand. In the long run, this will help you to make better choices in your life.

Be Proactive

The more aware you are of your power over your own choices, the more capable you will be of changing the course of your life. You cannot change others' behavior, but you have a lot of power to make changes in your own life.

No one is going to make things better *for* you. You have to do this all by yourself. Sometimes people think that if they marry the right person, she or he will take care of them and their lives will work out perfectly. No such thing! *You* are responsible for your life. Nobody else can do it for you. Perhaps the 11 most important words in the English language are: "If it is to be, it is absolutely up to me."

When you have a problem, ask yourself: "How would I like to feel about this experience?" By thinking specifically about how you want to feel you can then create a "future rehearsal," which is a detailed description of the way you would like to feel about the experience *as if* it were happening now. For example: "I am on the job interview. I am dressed in my favorite navy blue suit and my hair is styled the way I like it. I am comfortable and confident and I have my list of questions with me. I believe that I can do this job and I can do well on this interview!"

"It always seems impossible until it's done."

—Nelson Mandella

Organize Your Life for Success

In his bestselling book, *The Seven Habits of Highly Effective People*, Dr. Stephen Covey describes a very useful way to look at your life and organize it for success. He recommends that you be proactive by developing a vision of your mission, in the process of deciding what is most important to accomplish.

By prioritizing in this way, you make clear distinctions among the following four situations:

- URGENT AND IMPORTANT: crises that must be dealt with immediately;
- URGENT BUT NOT IMPORTANT: things that still have to be dealt with right away;
- **NOT URGENT, BUT IMPORTANT**: things that you need to stay on top of; and
- NOT IMPORTANT AND NOT URGENT.

Take another look at the third bullet. When you regularly pay very close attention to those things that are **NOT URGENT BUT IMPORTANT,** you avoid a lot of problems and accomplish a great deal. Some examples are as follows: getting the oil changed for your car, replacing furnace filters, paying your bills, doing the laundry, keeping the refrigerator well stocked, talking with your child about his/her day, getting the office report finished by the deadline and scheduling annual physical exams.

Another benefit of prioritizing is it gives you a chance to clarify your thinking so that you are creating a better picture for yourself of what is most important for you.

The Power of Smiling

Have you ever been walking along, thinking about something that is fun or humorous, and suddenly realize that you're smiling? Did you notice, then, that other people were smiling back at you? Smiling is contagious! Practice smiling and notice all of the smiles coming in your direction. Your smile can light up someone else's life as well as your own.

Current neuroscience research on positive thinking and gestures verifies that smiling lights up mirror neurons in your brain and stimulates uplifting chemicals in your body. These biochemical shifts help to create a happier mood. Since everyone mirrors everyone else, this mechanism multiplies when you smile. In one study at Harvard University, researchers asked doctors and other healthcare professionals to smile and make more eye contact with patients. The changes from just that one action were astounding and facilitated better communication and positive impact. For further reading on this subject read Shawn Achor's book, *The Happiness Advantage: The Seven Principles of Positive Psychology That Fuel Success and Performance at Work.*

We now know that the brain processes things singularly. In other words, it can devote its resources to only one thing at a time. If you focus on smiling while thinking a positive thought, that thought will expand and you will feel better. Simply by getting in the habit of smiling at other people, you are reinforcing your brain's ability to enhance your happiness.

So remember that when you smile, as the song goes: "the whole world smiles with you."

DAY 19

The Importance of Self-Talk

Your internal self-talk will determine your mood, behavior and feelings. In other words, how you think about and react to an event will affect how you feel. Your feelings will have a strong impact on whatever actions you take in any given situation.

According to the noted psychologist and author Dr. Albert Ellis, many times our first thought is the sensible one. But then our second thought is not always sensible and can be harmful. For example, you are working on reconciling with your husband after a difficult period in your marriage. You go on a lovely weekend outing and a pleasant hike. In the evening, you enjoy a delicious candle-lit dinner in a restaurant with great atmosphere overlooking a lake, and lots of cuddling. You are driving home, and when you are a half hour from home you get into a big argument about where you think your child would be happiest in college. Your first thought: "Our weekend was so good; maybe this small argument is manageable." But your second thought is, "I need to get out of this marriage; it will never work." That second thought comes from frustration and disappointment and is emotionally driven. Take a deep breath. Return to your first thought. It comes from clear thinking and a balanced mind.

For further reading on this topic read: *Overcoming Destructive Beliefs, Feelings and Behaviors*, by Dr. Albert Ellis.

Pausing, taking a deep breath and doing some meta-communicating about the situation can really help! Meta-communication means talking about the tone and meaning of the conversation that's going on "beneath" the content. For example: "We're snapping at each other. Let's take some time out." This gives you a chance to step away from the situation, analyze what happened and readjust your thinking.

Positive Self-Talk

An endless stream of negative internal dialogue can be extremely counter-productive. Negative messages might be repeating themselves over and over again without your conscious awareness. These messages harm your self-esteem and cause shame and guilt. The more aware you are of what's going on in your mind, the more you'll be able to alter your thinking.

If you readily believe your negative self-thoughts, your physical well-being can be compromised. Begin to challenge thoughts that are working against your well-being and replace them with supportive thoughts that help build your self-esteem and return you to a more balanced and peaceful state of mind.

The following is a four-step stress management process, called **SBRC** which is described in *The Wellness Book* by Herbert Benson, MD and Eileen Stuart, RN, MD. Try this useful technique:

- **STOP** your automatic thoughts before they have a chance to escalate.
- **BREATHE** deeply to release physical tension and slow yourself down.
- **REFLECT** on the issue by asking yourself: "What am I saying to myself that is driving these bad feelings? Is this truly a crisis? Will worrying just keep me upset?"
- **CHOOSE** how to respond to the stressful thoughts by challenging them and replacing them with believable, supportive statements. Now, write down the supportive statements. This should help you feel a lot better!

Viktor Frankl's Story of Hope

During World War II, Dr. Viktor Frankl was imprisoned in Nazi concentration camps for over three years. Many days he felt that he was living one small step away from death. Over time he managed to find meaning in the daily suffering that he endured, and was able to reframe this unspeakable tragedy into a kind of triumph. His enduring sense of spirituality and belief in a future helped him to hold onto a sense of human dignity.

In his book, *Man's Search for Meaning,* Dr. Frankl teaches his psychotherapeutic theory known as logotherapy, which he developed under dire circumstances in the camps where the rest of his family had perished. Despite his horrendous living conditions and multiple losses, he held tight to the belief that no one could take away his freedom to determine his own attitude and spiritual well-being.

Frankl created logotherapy to help himself and his fellow prisoners cope and survive. Logos is the Greek word for meaning. Logotherapy theorizes that we have freedom to find meaning under all circumstances, even the most horrible ones. To describe his theory in simple terms, Frankl developed an equation: D=S minus M, or Despair=Suffering minus Meaning.

To suffer with meaning changes the suffering. You may be suffering because of grief, the loss of a loved one or loss of a dream. You may be suffering because of an illness, or disappointment in yourself about something that you did and you want to make sense of it and move on. The objective is to have faith and hope in the future and to find meaning in every moment of life.

"Adversity is like a strong wind. It tears away from us all but the things that cannot be torn, so that we see ourselves as we really are."
—Arthur Golden

Viktor Frankl: Finding Meaning in Suffering

In the middle of the night, Dr. Frankl would secretly gather with groups of prisoners to study and discuss logotherapy, supporting them through their discovery of meaning in their lives. He believed that control of one's thoughts was the only thing that he and his fellow prisoners had to work with, and that understanding this power would make a huge contribution towards their survival.

When the war ended and Frankl's freedom was established, he began teaching logotherapy to his psychiatry patients. The following is an example of how one of his patients used his teachings to develop meaning in her life despite her difficult circumstances:

A very spirited and determined quadriplegic patient of Dr. Frankl's (she was paralyzed from the neck down), wrote with a pencil in her mouth because she could not use her hands to write. Whenever she read a news article about someone who was suffering, she sent them a letter of hope and encouragement by telling them about her situation and how she was coping with it. By reaching out to others on a daily basis, this woman gave deep meaning to her own suffering and severe physical challenges.

"That some good can be derived from every event is a better proposition than that everything happens for the best, which it assuredly does not."
—James K. Feibleman

Create Your Own Destiny

Some people believe that we don't create our own destiny. Yes, many things happen to us over which we have no control. At the same time, we can actively manage and improve many aspects of our lives.

I once worked with a man whom I will call Joe. He felt sorry for himself a lot of the time. He had been abused both physically and mentally as a child and now, at the age of 40, he had been married and divorced twice, had no children and few friends. He was lonely and felt others were not treating him well. In each situation in life, Joe saw only the negative aspects and he felt terribly stuck. His chronically distrustful outlook and continuous disappointments caused his body to experience stress, which in turn created chronic physical pain. Even when people were kind to him, he would notice one small negative issue, enlarge it in his mind and cancel out their good intentions.

Now, Joe was determined to emerge from behind the protective wall that he'd built so many years ago. As we worked together, he gradually began to see that there were two parts of himself: One part was willing to give people a break, take some risks and say "yes" to life. The other part wanted to stay crouched behind his fortress and remain bitter. I suggested he see his situation as: "the one hand and the other hand." The right hand was the stubborn, untrusting one that needed a lot of nurturing and encouragement. The left hand was the braver, more self assured one.

In time, Joe began to emerge from his tight cocoon. The more self-assured part of him began to take charge of his life and develop increasing confidence. For example, he started doing some Internet dating. With each rejection—an inevitable part of online dating—he was able to work through the issues and build on his courage rather than automatically, bitterly withdraw from the dating process. In time, he met a woman with whom he was able to establish a long-term relationship. After eight months, that relationship ended. Instead of being devastated by it, Joe analyzed the situation realistically, determined that they were not a truly compatible couple, and was able to move on. He began to see that indeed he could create his own destiny, and expect to change no one in the world but himself.

"Life is the sum of all of your choices."

—Albert Camus

Give Life a Chance

My client Miriam had a cousin, Laura, who suffered severe PMS (premenstrual syndrome). One morning, Laura awakened with a particularly severe episode of PMS, became deeply depressed and drowned herself in the ocean. Miriam, who knew her cousin well, was convinced that if Laura had been able to call for help that day, she never would have ended her life. Miriam believed that by sunrise the next day, her cousin would have felt strong enough to continue living.

Sometimes, pain and depression can be overwhelming. If this is the case for you, it is important to seek help immediately. With the help of a doctor or other health professional, you can explore anti-depressant medications, which can be extremely helpful in relieving depression. Sometimes, a small dose of medication can help you feel calmer and have a much better perspective on your experiences. But it is important to combine this with talk therapy so that you can sort out the issues that are contributing to your depression and learn how to better navigate your life.

"The art of living lies less in eliminating our troubles than in growing with them."

—**Bernard M. Baruch**

Beware of "Halt:" Hungry, Angry, Lonely, Tired

Many powerful self-help tools have been developed by Alcoholics Anonymous. One of them is the acronym **HALT,** which can remind you to become aware of four emotional and physical conditions. If you ignore them, trouble is around the corner because you can relapse into negative thinking.

HUNGRY: Notice when you are hungry. Bring small nourishing snacks with you when you leave the house, keep your blood sugar level stable, and don't skip meals. When you bring along your own food, you won't be tempted to eat junk food and snacks out of hungry desperation.

ANGRY: Anger is an appropriate emotion. It sends out a red flag warning when something is not right in your life. However, expressing anger is different from acting on it. If you act out your anger against yourself or others, you can create a very negative situation. It is important to say what is on your mind, but equally important to say it with calm presence and self-control.

LONELY: In the past, you may have isolated yourself to cope with life's problems. But if you're still doing it on a regular basis, it's a danger signal. Try to stay connected with people. Consider calling a friend or relative now and then, or setting up a museum date or a lunch date. Think about joining a choir, a church, a senior center or taking a class in something that interests you. Current studies show that the human brain is a social organ. We are meant to be with others. Regular communication builds upon a healthy, more balanced life.

TIRED: Get enough sleep, naps, rest, and don't overdo. Sometimes finding a quiet moment in your day to just close your eyes for five minutes and take a break from it all can be very helpful. Once or twice a week, try going to bed a little earlier than usual; that can help you a lot, too.

DAY 26

Go for It!

Before going on a date, to a party, a meeting, a family gathering or other occasion, think to yourself: "Things will work out wonderfully." This suggestion makes me think of a friend who regularly said: "I feel great today!"

These kinds of positive statements can be very powerful. The brain moves in the direction that you tell it to go. As with a bow and arrow, face the target and point the arrow in the direction that you are targeting. When the direction says: "I feel great today," your mind, body and spirit will move in that direction. Chances are, you *will* have a wonderful day! But don't believe me—try it!

"Find a place (inside yourself) where there is joy, and the joy will burn out the pain."

—Joseph Campbell

So much of life is the process, the journey itself. It is not so much about looking for the one large or small thing that might or might not exist. It is about living truly in the present. Don't carry around the weight of yesterday or the worries of tomorrow. Set up your life so that you live in your very own 24 hour cycle. Sir William Osler called that: "Living in day-tight compartments."

"Learning too soon our limitations, we never learn our powers."
—Mignon McLaughlin

What could be holding you back might not be the person you are, but the person you think you are not. The only way to find out who you are is to learn about yourself on a day-to-day basis and make room for a belief in yourself to grow and develop.

DAY 27

Learn to Self-Soothe

When bad things happen, it is natural for anxiety to be flowing throughout your body. As mentioned previously when anxiety rises, your brain readies you to fight or flee, just like your ancestors in the cave days. Your heart rate and breathing speed up, and your muscles tighten. Afterward, mental pictures of the dreaded experience, feelings and even sounds and smells may repeat themselves over and over again in your mind. This is how flashbacks develop.

For example, someone breaks into your house while you are away for the weekend, and when you get home you find that some things are missing and others are in disarray. Even though you make a police report, clean everything up and file a claim with your insurance company, you find that you still have flashbacks about that horrible experience.

It is not the robbery itself that causes the symptoms, but your responses to the event. Your brain remains stuck in survival mode. Your symptoms could include flashbacks, panic, restlessness, concentration problems, memory lapses, insomnia, irritability, loss of appetite and depression.

You need to create an alliance with your body in order to help it heal from the traumatic experience. Take several deep breaths as you say to yourself: "I am safe now." Then imagine what you will be doing in the coming weeks to make the situation better and better for yourself. You might decide to put locks on the windows or put in a security system. Know that the feelings of panic usually come in waves. Allow the waves to come and know that they will subside. Then they will come again and subside again.

You can also do some guided imagery to help calm yourself. Try to use all of your senses as you create an imaginary scene. Take a deep breath, and imagine being in a place that helps you to feel safe and comfortable.

It may be the beach, in the mountains, or somewhere in your house or on your porch, perhaps sitting with a good friend, relative or a beloved pet. As you imagine the scene, notice the details. If your safe place is at the beach, for example, notice the colors, imagine soaking in the sun on your skin, hear the waves, experience the breeze touching your skin, smell the ocean. This process will help you to become relaxed and in control of your life once again.

Belleruth Naparstek's book *Invisible Heros: Survivors of Trauma and How They Heal* offers many examples of guided imagery. Belleruth has also produced excellent guided imagery audio materials available on Healthjourneys.com. You might want to consider reading: *Tapping In: A Step-by-Step Guide To Activating Your Healing Resources Through Bilateral Stimulation* by Laurel Parnell, Ph.D. This is an excellent resource that can be very helpful with overcoming the effects of trauma.

See it, Believe it: Visualization and Guided Imagery

Dr. Maxwell Maltz's *Psycho Cybernetics* is a classic self help book written in the 1960s that is extremely helpful for reframing thought processes. Dr. Maltz states that we have to clear out old negative data from our minds in order to make room for new positive thoughts. Through the practice of visualization you can develop the ability to enhance these positive thoughts.

"Life isn't about finding yourself. Life is about creating yourself."
—George Bernard Shaw

When you create an imaginary scene in your mind, you engage the right side of your brain. This part of the brain taps into sensations, emotions and creativity, while the left side of the brain focuses on thinking and analyzing. Try this: Bring up the face of a loved one in your mind. Use it as a resource for self-soothing to get you through a hard day. Each time you feel stress, imagine this face smiling gently at you.

Get in the habit of taking mini-breaks throughout the day. Take a deep breath and just be in the present moment. Close your eyes. Notice that you are safe now. You are okay. Try not to think of past regrets or future plans. Just be here now. Then take several more deep breaths.

If you have a few more minutes, do a brief guided imagery. Close your eyes. You might imagine yourself in the woods surrounded by lovely trees. Experience the earth beneath your feet as you walk on a quiet path. Breathe in the fresh air. Smell the scent of evergreens. Take some cleansing breaths.

Now, open your eyes. This brief respite will help you to relax and clear your mind for creativity.

"To exist is to change; to change is to mature; to mature is to go on creating one's self endlessly."

—Henri Bergson

Keeping a Journal

Keeping a journal offers you the opportunity to make fuller sense of your life. It gives your unique story shape, structure and meaning as it evolves over the years. Through journaling, you will develop a kind of intimacy with yourself. This level of self-awareness is grounding and supportive and will allow you to feel part of the world.

Put down a full date next to all of your entries including the year. You will find this to be especially helpful in the future when reviewing the information.

When you journal, put your editor in the back seat. Shrug off the rules. Don't try to write things down perfectly. This work is between you and yourself and no one else, unless you choose to share it. Write from your heart and write frequently. Journaling is free self-therapy!

Through writing, you'll gain a deeper understanding of your true self—the person you really are, not the one you should be. Stop "should-ing" on yourself and start living *your* life. Understand your true wants and needs. By writing things down, you'll be able to move negative emotions out of your body and onto the page. Give yourself permission to acknowledge all of your feelings.

If something is weighing on your mind, write about it before going off to sleep so the thoughts don't keep you awake. Use journaling for problem solving, too. It is a very versatile tool!

If you wish, record brief descriptions of your dreams. Put a star next to dreams so that you can identify them easily within the body of the page.

You will find many helpful books on journal writing. Here are a few: *Writing for Your Life* by Deena Metzger; *Journal to the Self: 22 Paths to Personal Growth*, by Kathleen Adams and *The New Diary: How to use a Journal for Self-Guidance and Expanded Clarity* by Tristine Ranier.

Journal for Self-Understanding

History will grow out of your journaling and a record of your life will begin developing on the pages. You might want to share some of this with you children or other family members in your later years.

"We write to taste life twice; in the moment and in retrospect."
—Anais Nin

Journaling will help you heal by connecting with parts of yourself that you left behind when you were swept in the whirlwind of everyday life. It will help calm your mind and body and keep you grounded in the present.

I remember once receiving some shocking news about a family member. I was very distraught and didn't know what to do. At the time there was no one to talk to so I took out my journal and began to write. I found this to be very soothing and helpful. It truly calmed me down and helped me to find clarity.

Create New Behaviors

At times, you might want to create a new behavior, or redevelop a long-forgotten one. The following technique can help you accomplish this:

Select a behavior that you want to develop. For example, you decide to look on the brighter side of life more often.

Think of when and where you want to be able to do this behavior. For example, you may want to use it at work.

Identify a role model who exhibits the behavior in a way that you admire. As you picture that person doing this behavior, begin to think about how you might mimic it.

Find a comfortable place to sit or lie down. Take three deep, slow, cleansing breaths. Allow your entire body to relax. Now, make mental images of your role model exhibiting the behavior. See it as if it were a moving picture in your mind. Notice the person's body movements, posture, facial expressions and what he or she is saying.

Now, replace the role model with yourself and see *yourself* in the movie behaving like the expert behaves.

Imagine yourself stepping inside of the picture doing the chosen behavior. Feel your body as you experience the new behavior.

Now do what is known as a "future rehearsal," whereby you see yourself experiencing this new behavior in a future situation.

I've used this practice myself to help develop a new behavior. My mother had a wonderful sense of humor. In the last few years of her life I had a chance to spend a lot of time with her. After she died, I thought a lot about her and used the above technique to further develop my own sense of humor. Not only did it work, but it also gave me another way to remain connected to her.

This concept and many others like it, grew out of Neurolinguistic Programming. Some excellent books on the topic are: *Heart of the Mind: Engaging your Inner Power with NLP*, by Connierae Andreas and Steve Andreas; *Beliefs*, by Robert Dilts, Tim Hallbom and Suzi Smith and *Frogs Into Princes,* by Richard Bandler, John Grindler and John O. Stevens.

Do a Little Each Day

"There are so many things that we wish we had done yesterday, so few that we feel like doing today."

—Mignon McLaughlin

I once had a client who wanted to clear her office at work and make it more manageable. She had hundreds of magazines lined up on shelves that she did not need. I recommended that she place 5 magazines in the recycle bucket a day. She did this and told me that this meant that she was recycling 25 magazines a week, and 100 magazines a month.

After three months she had recycled about 300 magazines and felt much better about her office space. It took her exactly one minute a day to complete this project. But if she had tried to eliminate 300 magazines at one time, she would have been overwhelmed because she had a very complex, busy job and had neither the time to pack up all of the magazines nor the physical strength to carry heavy boxes. So this technique worked very well for her. By working on a small amount of her project each day, she was developing new neural pathways for the new habit. The key was to keep it up every day for only one or two minutes. Doing a little bit each day can make a huge difference!

"Motivation is what gets you started. Habit is what keeps you going."
—Milton Erickson, MD

Whatever you put your energy into will become your life. Take some time out to notice how you actually spend your time each day. These days build up to many weeks, then many months and then many years. By becoming conscious of your activities and analyzing them on a day-to-day basis, you will eventually find that you are actually changing your life—and moving it in the direction that you want it to go.

"How we spend our day is of course, how we spend our lives."
—Annie Dillard

The Ten Minute a Day Commitment

"It does not matter how slowly you go so long as you do not stop."
—Confucius

"Success is a matter of understanding and religiously practicing specific, simple habits that lead to success."

—Robert J. Ringer

If there is a project that you want to get involved in but can't seem to stick with, try making a ten-minute-per-day commitment to it. That will get you in the "ballpark." For example, if you like to play the guitar but haven't picked it up in years, spend ten minutes a day playing. By the end of the week you'll have put in 70 minutes—on something that, just a week ago, you couldn't seem to get started on.

One of my clients wanted to get back into her ceramics project. She had abandoned it for six years and a stack of unfinished vases were sitting in the closet collecting dust. She felt that she didn't have the time to do it justice then, but the years continued to roll along. I recommended that she take out one vase and work on it for ten minutes a day. As a result of this, she was able to once again move forward in her ceramic painting, from which she derived a great deal of pleasure.

As previously mentioned when you develop a new habit, you build tracks in your brain in the form of new neural pathways. As you repeat the new habit over and over again, you are deepening that learning track. As the new neural pathways are established, it becomes easier and easier to go back to the project on a regular basis and stay with it.

"Begin doing what you want to do now. We are not living in eternity. We have only this moment, sparkling like a star in our hand and melting like a snowflake."

—William Wordsworth

How to Get the Job Done

"Until you value yourself, you won't value your time. Until you value your time you will not do anything with it."

—M. Scott Peck

Do you ever find that you want to do something, but every time you think about it you get overwhelmed and don't do it? The issue doesn't go away. It just sits there somewhere in your life and takes up space, making you very uncomfortable.

David, a respiratory therapist needed a new computer to do research, write letters and do bookkeeping. He was also a parent and needed it for his children and their schoolwork. He came to our session berating himself about being "lazy," terribly stuck and quite depressed because he couldn't get motivated to purchase the computer.

I asked him what he specifically needed in a computer. He told me that he needed a word processor, wireless capacity, specific software, and a few other items. I took out a 9x12 inch pad and asked him to write down each item as he described it to me. Based on this discussion, he decided to go to a local store to have a needs assessment done, order the equipment and arrange to have it installed. I then asked David to provide a date by which he planned to complete the project, and suggested that he put all of it on his calendar. When I saw him again in three weeks, the computer was up and running.

It is extremely helpful to write down exactly what you need and set up a deadline by which you will have the job completed. David had frequently thought about what he needed but had never written it down, so it was all running around in his head. The more it ran around, the more overwhelmed he became. By writing it down, he developed a "road map" for himself, and then followed it.

Remember: If you dream it, you can do it,—but you need a deadline!

"If you take too long deciding what to do with your life, you'll find you've done it."

—**Pam Shaw**

Take a Chance

"Life is like fording a river, stepping from one slippery stone to another, and you must rejoice every time you don't lose your balance, and learn to laugh at the times you do."

—Merle Shain

In this wonderful quote, Merle Shain, author of *Hearts That We Broke Long Ago,* reminds us that life is filled with one "issue" or problem after another. Some days you think that things are going smoothly and then suddenly something unexpectedly troublesome occurs. During those times, it's helpful to step back, take a deep breath, and say to yourself: "this too shall pass." Reframe the problem as a "temporary inconvenience." Then start doing some practical troubleshooting to work on the issue at hand.

Some problems may relate to discouraging past events that get in the way of your continuing personal growth. If you seem to be stuck in the past, try the technique of switching your thoughts to "future gear" through imagery and pairing of positive experiences with new learnings.

For example, Isabel wanted to take ice skating lessons, but every time she thought about attempting this new skill, she shied away from the idea. At the age of nine, she'd taken a clumsy fall on the ice and experienced excruciating embarrassment. Her so-called friends had made fun of her and called her "klutzy." Being a sensitive child, the discomfort of this experience embedded itself in her developing sense of self and remained there.

I asked Isabel to switch gears and think of a time when she'd felt a lot of confidence. She described feeling very proud of a speech that she recently presented at an important work-related meeting. Then I asked her to get in touch with how that confidence felt in her body. She reported that her entire core had a solid, grounded sensation. Her legs felt sturdy, and a light, flowing energy spread throughout her entire body.

Next, I asked Isabel to picture herself ice skating and at the same time bring up that strong sense of confidence throughout her body. She closed her eyes and created a pairing of the two experiences. I then asked her to continue to imagine herself skating around and around and then to notice what she did when she fell. She imagined falling on the ice and picking herself up and continuing to skate, surging ahead with a big smile on her face, totally ignoring the remarks of her peers. This is what we call a "future rehearsal," as mentioned before, in which a person sees herself in the future experiencing positive feelings while engaged in a new activity. This gave Isabel the confidence to take ice skating lessons that she went on to enjoy thoroughly.

Letting Go of the Past

"As your understanding of life continues to grow, you can walk upon this planet safe and secure, always moving forward towards your greater good."

—Louise L. Hay

If you are experiencing negativity with people on a regular basis and you find that you are very irritable about what appears to be small situations, you may be carrying some past baggage with you. The better you understand yourself and what drives your behavior, the happier and more at peace you will be.

I once had a client, Ben, who was still in a lot of emotional pain nine years post-divorce. Although he and his ex-wife did not have any children, he had a very difficult time moving on. As we explored this painful issue, one of the things that surfaced was related to his father. Apparently, his father knew that Ben's wife was planning to leave him, but he didn't tell Ben that he was aware of it. Ben felt doubly betrayed. Over time the relationship between father and son became distant, stilted and full of unexpressed tension.

When Ben brought up this sensitive issue in therapy, his father had been deceased for many years, so he was unable to ask his father why he didn't tell him about the impending separation and why he was unsupportive towards his son at that time. As we moved along in therapy, other issues between father and son surfaced such as his father's pressuring Ben to be athletic and not supporting his passion for music.

My client felt that he could not trust anyone, especially those closest to him. He felt stuck and in pain. This pain manifested itself in many of his relationships. He was always waiting for the next shoe to fall.

After several months of regular therapy, Ben wrote a letter to his father describing his pain concerning this and other issues. This was a turning point for him. Although he could not hand the letter to his father, just the act of writing it and sorting out the issues freed him from his inner turmoil. Over a period of time Ben was able to process many unfinished issues and concerns from his past. This helped him to feel more at peace with himself. Over a period of time he developed the ability to be more open and trusting with others. Dr. Francine Shapiro's book *Getting Past Your Past; Take Control of Your Life With Self-Help Techniques From EMDR Therapy* is an extremely useful resource for helping you with these issues.

"The world is full of suffering; it is also full of overcoming."
—Helen Keller

Stages of Change

Dr. Virginia Satir developed a model entitled "Stages of Change," which describe the steps that people take when they confront a significant life change.

We begin with the **Status Quo** which is the predictable, the known. It could be the job you've had for seven years, the one that you felt that you were outgrowing two years ago. As the desire for change emerges within you, fear erupts and you continue to stay on the job. After awhile, you feel so deeply locked into the uncomfortable situation that you become ready to take the leap in order to dislodge your feet from the cement!

But once you actually make the move, you're dealing with the introduction of a **Foreign Element**—in this case, a new job. At this point, many facets of your life suddenly change. You may have a new commute to deal with, new co-workers, a totally new job description and many other small and large changes.

These multiple new challenges thrust you into **Chaos.** Your feet are no longer in cement but they are dangling in mid-air because many changes are occurring all at once in your life. Feeling insecure and out of control, you may wonder, "Why did I do this to myself?"

After a while a "settling-in" phase begins to develop, as you gain competence in your new job and familiarity with your new surroundings. This phase of consolidating new learnings is known as **Integration.**

Now you are ready to fully **Practice** this new state of being that you've created. Repeated practice reinforces the fresh learnings and new neural pathways are strengthened. You are now entering **A New Status Quo**, and now the cycle begins again.

These Stages of Change will continue throughout your life. The steps are predictable and can be applied to most changes in your life. Understanding them can give you a road map that will provide a sense of predictability. The first time around can be the most difficult, but as you have more experience with change, the steps are likely to become easier, and assist you on your journey. For more information on this topic read: *The Satir Model, Family Therapy and Beyond*, by Virginia Satir, John Banemen, Jane Gerber, and Maria Gomori.

"If one were to give an account of all the doors one has closed and opened, all the doors one would like to re-open, one would have to retell the story of one's entire life."

—Gaston Bachelard

Organizing Your Psychological Closet

Change is inevitable. The more fully we accept this reality, the smoother the journey will be. But learning how to gracefully live with the constant changes that life brings us can be a daunting challenge. Psychotherapist Virginia Satir invented the concept of the "Psychological Closet" to help us cope with the constancy of change. She asks us to compare our clothes closet to a psychological closet.

When you are ready for a new wardrobe, you usually buy a few new outfits and keep the old ones for a while. After getting accustomed to your new "look," you begin to give away old outfits that no longer work for you.

In the same way, you keep plenty of habits in your psychological closet. When you decide to develop new habits, don't try to give up the old ones. Just move them a little further back in your psychological closet. Now, start working on developing the new ones. In time, you'll be ready to let the old habits fade away.

When it comes to change, it's often more comfortable to think in terms of adding something new before removing the old and familiar. For example, instead of thinking in terms of losing weight, try thinking about small ways to add more nourishing food to your diet. Or, if you don't like your negative attitude, consider being more mindful of what you say and adding one positive statement to your vocabulary each day.

"Life is a process of becoming, a combination of states we have to go through. Where people fail is that they wish to elect a state and remain in it."

—Anais Nin

"The problem is not that there are problems. The problem is expecting otherwise, and thinking that having problems is a problem."
—Theodore Rubin

Virginia Satir created many beautiful metaphors like the "Psychological Closet." For further readings on this and related topics you might want to explore: *Meditations of Virginia Satir, Peace Within, Peace Between, Peace Among,* Edited by Dr. John Banemen and *Making Contact,* by Dr. Virginia Satir.

Getting Comfortable with Change

"It is the most unhappy people who most fear change."
—Mignon McLaughlin

This is a very interesting quote. In essence, the author states that if you fear change and hold yourself back based on that fear, you will be unhappy. The flip side of that coin is that, by acting courageously, you will find happiness as you move beyond fear and push yourself to grow.

"When we walk to the edge of all the light we have and take the step into the darkness of the unknown, we must believe that one of two things must happen: there will be something solid for us to stand on or we will be taught to fly."
—Patrick Overton

In this quote the writer assures us that as we take risks and endure challenges we will somehow survive—and perhaps even thrive.

"I keep the telephone of my mind open to peace, harmony, health, love and abundance. Then, whenever doubt, anxiety or fear try to call me, they keep getting a busy signal—and they'll soon forget my number."
—Edith Armstrong

As we've discussed, whatever you put energy into will become your life. Be proactive. When you decide on a true priority, go for it! Make a plan to reach your goal. And remember, attach a deadline to your dreams so that you will see them through.

When you set out to accomplish a task, think about how good you will feel when it's all finished. In other words, consider it done!

You Have Choices

Instead of eating cereal every morning for breakfast, try strawberries and muffins once in awhile. This may seem like a simple and even superficial change, but as you go through your day, notice your choices. What you choose to do at any moment in time is important and, the more mindful you are about your choices, the better ones you will make. Everyday decisions and choices are what make up our lives. Inch by inch it's a cinch, mile by mile it's a trial, and choice by choice it is a life. So choose well.

If you know where you are going, your journey will be a lot easier. If you went to a travel agent and told her that you wanted to go on a trip, she would ask you where you wanted to go. If you said: "Well, I sure don't want to go to New York, and I know that I don't want to go to Mississippi," the travel agent would not be able to issue you a ticket. But if you said: "I want to go to Arizona," she would book the trip for you.

When I ask clients what they want, they often tell me what they want someone *else* to do. For example: "I want my husband to spend more time with our children". Or, they tell me what they don't want: "I don't want to keep coming in to work late every day."

But in order to create change, you have to 1) focus on your own behavior and 2) be proactive about it. When you figure out what it is that you truly want, state your goal in positive terms. For example: "I want to get up at 6:30 AM every weekday morning so that I have enough time to get ready for work and be there on time."

The brain works like a bow and arrow. It sets a target and moves in that direction. When you become very clear about what you want, you will be able to move directly towards your goal. This is an extremely important issue. So, to summarize the steps: first decide exactly what it is that you want, and then state it in the positive. A good thing to do at this point is to imagine yourself accomplishing the goal. Everything you do begins in your head. Now do as the bumper sticker says: "Go for it!"

As you develop more clarity about your needs, you will be better able to express them to others with certainty. As you do this on a regular basis, your overall satisfaction will greatly improve.

"Whether you think you can or think you can't, you're right."
—Henry Ford

Focus on the "Wins"

Do you find that when you have a project to do, you think of how much there is left to do and chastise yourself for not doing enough? Try a different tactic: notice how much you've already accomplished and give yourself a pat on the back for having done it! In other words, focus on the "wins."

For example, let's say you are reorganizing your closet. When you are about 20 minutes into the project, step back and observe what a nice job you've already done on the closet. This will give you the inspiration to keep going. Then be sure to take a break with a time limit on it. For example, give yourself a half hour to have a bite to eat. When you come back after the break you will feel refreshed and ready to move on with your project. Throughout the rest of the project, periodically become aware of what you have accomplished and give yourself credit for it.

Being compassionate with yourself will help you to more deeply enjoy and appreciate your life.

Dr. Virginia Satir asks us to imagine that we are ships at sea. We don't have any control over the weather. It might rain or the winds might toss us around. However, we do have some control over when and where we will take our ship.

In other words, you don't have control over how other people will respond to you, but you do have control over how to respond to them! Whenever someone sends you an invitation to get angry, remember that you don't have to accept their invitation. You can choose to respond in any way that is acceptable to you. It is important to be aware of what you can and cannot control.

THE SERENITY PRAYER

**God grant me the serenity
to accept the things I cannot change,
the courage to change the things I can,
and wisdom to know the difference.**
—Reinhold Niebuhr

The day I learned this prayer was a turning point for me, because its message has guided me throughout my life. I hope that it is helpful to you.

Relationships: The Art of Listening

The topics on the following pages apply to relationships with intimate partners. However, many aspects can also apply to relationships with coworkers, children, parents, friends, acquaintances and others in your life.

"No one has ever loved anyone the way everyone wants to be loved."
—Mignon McLaughlin

People want to be heard, understood, and acknowledged more than anything in the world. A really wonderful way to communicate is through active listening. It shows deep respect to the person you're conversing with.

Active listening involves repeating what you heard back to your partner. For example, your partner tells you that he thought that you were being disrespectful of him. Instead of getting defensive, the typical "knee jerk" reaction to criticism—ask him what he meant by "you were disrespectful of me." Let him explain it in his own words. Then repeat back what you heard. (Notice that you have to listen carefully in order to be able to do this!) Then ask him if you got it right. He might say: "Yes, that is what I meant." Do not defend yourself. Instead, ask him to describe more about his feelings. This will enable you to open up the issue and discuss it. Now, *you are responding rather than reacting* to him.

If you keep the goal of truly understanding your partner in the forefront of your mind, you will remain curious about how and why he sees you as behaving disrespectfully.

After doing this, you should reverse roles so that you get a chance to say how you feel about the issue, with his undivided attention and active listening.

While listening openly to criticism is hard to do, it is well worth the effort because it can enhance and enrich your relationship. After you have a sense of completion on this issue, give your communication practice a rest and involve yourselves in other activities, preferable something of a lighter nature. Some time later go through this exercise again with an issue or concern occurring in your relationship with him.

Relationships: How to Speak so Your Partner Listens

"Chains do not hold a marriage together. It is threads, hundreds of tiny threads which sew people together through the years. That is what makes a marriage last—more than passion or even sex."
—Simone Signoret

Regular day-to-day loving, respectful interactions have the capacity to hold a relationship safe, secure and peaceful. Still, no matter how hard you work on harmony, there will be times when you and your partner get stuck in a negative interaction. It is best at those times to arrange to sit together, face each other and talk it out. Take the time to really listen to each other. When you approach your partner in an appreciative and welcoming manner, miracles can happen!

Pick your battles. Some things are not worth fighting about and in those cases it is best to simply "look the other way." If you make a fuss about everything that comes up, your partner will tune you out. There has to be a balance. As you get to know your needs and your partner's needs better, you will learn where that balance is located.

There are some issues that seem to be unsolvable and therefore require a lot of compromise. One way to deal with this is to try to stay "current" and don't let issues build up.

It is important to talk out the hard issues. Timing is crucial. You don't want to talk about a very difficult concern when you are: angry, tired, hungry, in a hurry or on your way to work. You need to cool off, be rested, eat something, and don't have a deadline or a pressing job in front of you. When possible, it's good to actually make an appointment to settle a disagreement.

Keep in mind that your main goal is to gain a deeper understanding of your partner, yourself and your situation. Watch your language and be respectful of each other.

Remember, the above suggestions also apply to relationships with co-workers, children, parents, friends and other important people in your life.

Some excellent books on relationships include: *Getting the Love You Want,* by Harville Hendrix, Ph.D.; *The Seven Principles for Making Marriage Work,* by John M. Gottman, Ph.D. and Nan Silver.

Relationships: Be Respectful

"Respect is love in plain clothes."

—Merle Schain

When possible use "I" messages instead of "You" messages. For example, don't say: "You always yell out to me from the other room and don't take the time to come inside and talk to me in person." Instead, try: "I am uncomfortable when you yell out to me from the other room. But I do want to hear what you have to say. Let's work out a compromise that will work for both of us." In the second statement, you are taking responsibility for your own feelings, not making accusations. You are also offering a complaint with a request attached to it. This opens the door to the possibility of productively resolving the problem instead of just complaining about it. Taking the time to improve the way you speak to each other can be extremely helpful towards the development of a loving, harmonious relationship.

Whenever possible, do not raise your voice. If your voice is calm, your partner's voice is likely to be calm, too. But if you raise your voice, you're inviting him/her to react in kind, and then you're off and running in a negative direction! If your discussion gets too hot and you are stuck, take some time out. Sometimes you need to end a discussion before it is completely resolved. You might need time to mull over the issues on your own and get back to each other when things are calmer. But don't wait too long. Unresolved issues can become more problematic if they are ignored. Maintain a positive physical appearance. Take a few minutes to comb you hair and freshen up before seeing you partner. This will perk you up. It also shows respect for your partner. People who live together sometimes get too casual with their appearance. Remember how hard you worked to appear attractive when you first met?

Dr. David Viscott encouraged us to start any complaint with the words: "I am uncomfortable...." I have found these three little words to be extremely helpful and I predict that you will, too. By saying them, you are giving yourself a chance to experience what is going on in the moment, to pause, and slow down the discussion. Then you can explain what is happening with you and ask your partner what is going on with her/him.

Don't let a "stamp collection" of complaints build up inside of you. Sometimes people collect stamps and put them in books. Collecting negative thoughts, feelings and experiences in your internal book can be a dangerous practice. It is best to deal with issues page by page and not get in the habit of throwing the book at your partner!

Dr. David Viscott wrote many excellent books that were filled with wisdom and valuable information about relationships. Among them are: *I Love You, Let's Work It Out.* and *The Viscott Method.*

Relationships: Nurture Your Bond

"Love is like a fragile flower."

—-Dr. David Viscott

It is so easy to get caught up in day-to-day activities and the busy-ness of life. You forget to look into each others' eyes and really notice each other, the way you once did. Think back to what brought you together in the first place. Reminiscing about how you met and what attracted you to each other will move you into another time zone—the time of the past when things were so different! That can open up new possibilities.

When I ask couples to tell me about what attracted them to each other, I often hear them say: "He (she) made me laugh." That is such an important thing, to be able to help someone experience the humor and zaniness of life! Often when sexual energy is high, the laughter comes easily. When you find yourself lost in the thicket of a troubled relationship, you want to find a way to step out of those woods and into the sunshine of hope. Reminiscing about the past, those early first dates, can be a very helpful tool to assist you in finding your way back home.

I have seen couples who feel they're in a rut and want to add new activities to their relationships—but have trouble getting started. Sometimes I will ask each person to write down ten things that they would like to do together. For example: take a trip to the zoo, go to a movie, have dinner out, take a train into town and visit a museum, go for a walk in the park, worship together, play tennis, go to a baseball game, go to a concert, and so on. I ask them to cut out each item on the list, put it in a jar and then, once a week, pick out a piece of paper from the jar. Whatever activity is on the paper is the one they'll do that day. This helps them to get into positive, enriching activities and feel more hopeful about their relationship.

Relationships: Small Acts of Love

People often think that once they say "I do" the relationship will work by itself and continue running smoothly. When you first buy a brand new car it runs quite well and usually doesn't need maintenance or repair. But after a while it can break down if you don't attend to it regularly. It is the same with a business. You have to pay attention to all aspects of it in order for it to remain successful. And so it is with relationships.

Once a week, set aside time to be alone together and have a "date" in order to remember where the spark is located! That will give you the strength to deal with problems when they come marching up to your doorstep.

Notice the little things that your partner does. Psychotherapist Richard Stuart developed a technique called "Caring Days." In this exercise, your wishes become your partner's *top priority* and visa versa. First, each of you creates a wish list of thoughtful acts that you think your partner would appreciate—things that you are easily able to fulfill. The list should contain ten or more items. Small gestures work well, such as buying her flowers, making coffee for him, washing her car, a foot massage for him, and so on.

The next step is to ask your partner whether the list fits their needs. Then assign "caring days" for each day of the week (for example, partner one takes Monday, partner two takes Tuesday, etc.) On your assigned day, do one thing for your partner from the list. At the end of that day, your partner has to guess what you did for him. Then on your partner's day, they will do one thing for you that is on the list.

This is a simple exercise that gets you thinking about each other in a positive way on a daily basis. After two weeks take the time to discuss how it went. If you both like the way it is working, make up another list.

The more effort you put into your relationship, the more benefits you will receive from it.

You will find "Caring Days" in Richard Stewart's book: *Helping Couples Change: A Social Learning Approach to Marital Therapy.*

"A new philosophy, a way of life, is not given for nothing. It has to be paid dearly for and only acquired with much patience and great effort."

—Fyodor Dostoyevsky

Relationships: Focus on the Big Picture

It is easy to get caught up in the small details and miss the big picture. Stay focused on your goal. If your goal is to be loving with your partner, keep that thought in your mind. What we think about is where we go. The brain is set up to move forward.

If you are wrong about something, admit it! An apology can go a long way towards a peaceful relationship. Don't let your pride get in the way.

"The doorknob of the heart opens from the inside."

—Meryl Shain

Stay away from using the terms "always" and "never." For example: "You always interrupt me when I am talking on the phone," or "You never tell me that I look nice." "Always" and "never" terms create an extreme version of negativity and they can shut out the possibility for healthy communication.

Tell your partner what you need. You might be thinking: "If she really loved me she would KNOW what I need." But that is incorrect. No one can ever really read your mind no matter who they are or how long they have known you. So, voice your wishes clearly. For example: "I would really love it if we could spend some time reading poetry to each other."

Robert Fulghum, author of *Everything I Need to Know I learned in Kindergarten*, wrote:

"...and it is still true, no matter how old you are, when you go out into the world it is best to hold hands and stick together."

We learn at an early age to hold hands when we cross the street. It is very helpful to have a hand to hold when crossing the streets of life. If someone close to you needs a medical procedure, or has to attend a challenging meeting, ask if they'd like you to accompany them. The moral support is very important. We want to feel that we are not alone in the world, especially during those scary times!

Another excellent book on relationships is: *Passage to Intimacy*, by Lori H. Gordon, Ph.D with Jon Frandsen.

DAY 48

Family:
Create a Healthy Environment

Family energy has a big impact on children. When parents are getting along and communicating well, the family atmosphere is calm. I once worked with a family of six who had lost a little girl in a car accident. For five years, the family grew apart. The wife had an affair, the husband got wrapped up in his job and the children were acting out in school. Finally, the parents decided to separate. At that point, the children began acting out even more. When this happened the mother decided to make some major changes. She ended her affair, stopped working, started staying at home and went into counseling.

The parents postponed their separation. They also had several family therapy sessions. As the mother dealt with all of the aspects of her losses in the present, past and distant past with her upbringing, she began to heal. Her husband then decided to go for treatment himself and put more energy into his family.

In time, all of the family members were able to talk about their pain concerning the loss of their beloved child and sister. As the parents began to connect in a much healthier way, the children calmed down and started to show signs of improvement at school. Ultimately, the couple did divorce but were able to remain kind and civil with each other and worked together as strong co-parents. This was immensely helpful to their children.

Parents who consciously reflect on their own lives and continue to grow are better able to support their children in a healthy manner.

"Every word, facial expression, gesture, or action on the part of a parent gives the child some message about self-worth. It is sad that so many parents don't realize what messages they are sending."
—Virginia Satir

Family: Stay in Communication

Dr. Virginia Satir's "Temperature Reading" is an excellent tool for families. In this exercise, everyone in the family is given a chance to air their complaints, state their concerns and offer new information. The structure of the "Temperature Reading" is very helpful in supporting good communication. It also can be used effectively in business settings. Following are the steps of the exercise:

APPRECIATIONS.

Two or three appreciations are expressed by each family member. Everyone needs to know that they are appreciated! Maybe you want to thank your 18-year-old daughter for being so kind to her grandfather last Friday when she drove him to the car dealership. Perhaps your seven-year-old son would like to express his thanks to his father for playing basketball with him last Saturday.

COMPLAINTS OR CONCERNS (WITH RECOMMENDATIONS).

Tell your family what is bothering you, but also be sure to state your recommendations for resolving the complaint. For example, you may have concerns about the very high electric bill this month. Be sure to make recommendations as to how this bill can be reduced and ask family members to offer their suggestions as well.

QUESTIONS OR PUZZLES.

Describe something that puzzles you. For example, your child may have told you that she has a soccer game but you don't remember whether it was to be Saturday or Sunday.

NEW INFORMATION.

For example, you may want to tell the family that Aunt Molly is coming for dinner on Sunday night at 7 p.m. and that you'd like everyone to arrange to be home at that time.

HOPES AND WISHES.

You might be wanting to set up a family vacation to the beach and would like to find out if others have similar interests.

Life-Space Diagram

Dr. Ray Bardill developed the "Life-Space Diagram," which provides the family with an opportunity to better understand what each person is feeling, what they need and how the relationships among the members can be improved.

Each family member draws a plain figure as follows: a rectangle, circle, square or triangle. Choose the figure that best represents you. For example, you might see yourself as a circle. Once you have chosen the figure, put your name inside of it.

The next step is to make a figure representing each family member, for example you might see your wife as a triangle and your son as a square. Put their names inside their figures, too. Now, place the figures in an order that reflects the way you experience the interactions among you now. For example, you may feel close to your wife, so you draw her close to you, but distant from your son, so you draw him further away from you, but you may believe that he is close to his mother, so you would draw him close to her.

Now, take another piece of paper and make another drawing of the same figures, but this time place them the way you would *like* them to be. For example, you might want to be closer to your son and you might want to become a triangle like your wife. So now you would change your figure into a triangle and move it closer to your son's figure. Be sure to put a name in each figure.

Now, write down what behaviors you feel you would have to change in yourself in order to make this overall change occur. For example, you may want to be involved in fewer activities outside of the home and become more available to your wife and son.

Each family member takes a turn with this exercise. Then they discuss their positions and their shapes. This can provide an opportunity for stronger understanding among family members.

"Seek first to understand the other person's position."
—Steven R. Covey

To Thine Own Self Be True

Sometimes it is a good idea to stop everything, close your eyes, go inside and tune in to your breathing. As you do this, really notice yourself and your feelings. "Stop the music," so to speak, and pause. You may find a lot of things bubbling up in your mind. Perhaps even things that you didn't realize were there! You may be denying something that you need to face. When you stop, breathe, and think you are able to make deep connections from within. Shakespeare had a very good point when he said: **"To thine own self be true."**

I was once working with a mother whose teenage son was having a very hard time coping with many challenges, especially those related to school and family. When the mother did this exercise, she became aware that her son's problems were much more serious than she had realized. This helped her to decide to seek professional help for him and for their family. She told me that up until that point, she had been in denial about this issue because she had been steeped in her busy day-to-day life. On this particular day she was ready to face the painful reality of the situation and be true to herself and her top priorities.

"Learn to get in touch with the silence within yourself and know that everything in this life has a purpose."

—Elizabeth Kubler-Ross

Build Your Internal Resources

Jessica was a history teacher who was also very handy around the house. But when confronted with a new "fix-it" challenge, she would invariably become overwhelmed. It was the uncertainty of the project's outcome that caused her anxiety. Although she had experience repairing everything from cars to toasters, each new project posed a threat to her peace of mind until she could meet the challenge.

The thing that finally helped her the most was writing a list of all of the things she had successfully repaired over the years and reading it to herself whenever she was confronted with an item in need of repair. She kept the list on top of the TV in the living room so that it was readily on hand. After reading the list, Jessica would tell herself that she could accomplish the new project for three reasons:

(1) she had a lot of experience (she listed fifteen things that she had successfully repaired and was very surprised to see how long her list was);
(2) if she ran into trouble, she had people with whom she could consult (she had listed those people's names) and
(3) when needed, she could hire helpers (she had also listed helpers that she could hire).

It is extremely helpful to be able build on your internal resources as Jessica did, so that you have confidence to move forward in your life in a focused, calm manner, despite any challenges that may come your way.

"I don't embrace trouble; that is as bad as treating it as an enemy. But I do say meet it as a friend, for you'll see a lot of it and had better be on speaking terms with it."

—Oliver Wendell Holmes

Believe in Your Uniqueness

Virginia Satir recommended that you wear an imaginary gold medallion around your neck. On one side of the medallion, in beautiful jeweled letters, an inscription reads: "Thank you for noticing me, what you ask fits for me, it is a Yes." On the other side of the medallion is an equally beautiful message: "Thank you for noticing me, what you ask does not fit for me, it is a No." Yes and No are equally beautiful. Consult your imaginary medallion for any situation in your life. By doing this, you will eventually get to know your true self and your unique needs.

Dr. Satir also recommended that you bow in front of your reflection in the mirror every day and say: "The world is a better place because I am here." There never was a "you" before and there never will be another "you" again! Your fingerprints prove it.

TIBETAN LEGEND

"There once was an old blind turtle who lived in the depths of the ocean. Once every 1000 years the turtle swam to the top of the sea and stuck its head up through the waves surfacing for air. Now imagine that there is a wooden ring floating on the surface of the ocean, and think of how rare it would be for the blind turtle coming up to the surface every 1000 years to put its head through the wooden ring. It is just that rare, say the Tibetans, for a being to gain human birth."

Get to Know the Gift of You

It is very important to take time every day to connect with yourself—to "check in" and see what you need to smooth out your day. You want to be sure that you are on the right track with everything that you are doing. If you are feeling down, get to the root of your problem and see what you need to do about it. Maybe you are lonely, if so, consider calling a friend. You might be overwhelmed. Take the time to find out what you need to become calmer and more confident. Imagine yourself as a plant that needs water from deep within it's roots in order to grow and thrive. Do whatever you need to do to nourish your plant.

It is important to notice your posture. Ann, my mother-in-law, used to say to me: "Stand tall!" She was right. When you feel bad, you might physically slump without being aware of it. By changing your posture, you'll change your mood. After all, the mind and body are one.

"The privilege of a lifetime is being who you are."
—Joseph Campbell

Virginia Satir recommended that you leave your judge's hat on the shelf at home and go into the world wearing your detective hat. Ask questions and don't assume anything.

When you want to make a change, be sure that you really want to do it. You might think that you want to do it, but deep down inside of you, there might be a lot of unanswered questions. The closer you get to what you really want, the more likely you will be to achieve it!

Practice Kindness

"What you meet in another being is the projection of your own level of evolution."

—Ram Dass

Joseph loved his wife but disliked being around his father-in-law. The older man had a gruff personality that reminded Joseph of an uncle that he disliked. Now, fifteen years into the marriage, Joseph and his father-in-law still had very little in common and often felt uncomfortable with each other. Joseph didn't want to invite his in-laws for Christmas dinner, but his wife urged him to do so. I suggested to Joseph that since his father-in-law was getting on in years, this would be a good time to make peace with himself concerning this man.

I recommended that he invite his in-laws to dinner, leave his judge's hat on the shelf, and wear his detective hat. I suggested that Joseph treat his wife's father civilly and with an extra touch of kindness just for himself and his own growth and healing. I used the metaphor of his life being like a piece of sculpture. As exquisite as it is, it still needs additional smoothing out around the edges. He gave this a lot of thought and decided that by exercising kindness and compassion with someone who has been a "thorn in his side" for many years, he would have an opportunity to grow and set a good example for his children. His wife would appreciate him more and it would add to the quality of their relationship. The gathering turned out very well, and Joseph was pleased not only with his own behavior but with his father-in-law's positive responses towards him. After awhile, Joseph began to see that this man was not his uncle, and that helped him to soften his reaction to his wife's father.

"Three things in human life are important. The first is to be kind. The second is to be kind, and the third is to be kind."

—Henry James

Step Outside of Yourself

Several years ago, I was a guest speaker at a Separated and Divorced Catholics group meeting in the Washington D.C. area. The topic was how to cope with the holidays when you are struggling with separation and divorce. Many people experience a great deal of emotional pain during the holiday season, which is magnified when they see so many people around them who appear to be happily connected with loved ones. The sense of isolation and loneliness can be overwhelming.

One man at the meeting shared a story that I will never forget. It was the first Christmas since his wife had left him and he was extremely sad. He decided to volunteer at a shelter for homeless people that day. He took the train from suburban Maryland into Washington D.C. and set to work serving turkey, stuffing and all of the holiday delicacies for a late afternoon dinner. He talked with the temporary residents of the shelter, sang along with the guitar music that was provided by another volunteer and played gin rummy with four men.

When he left the building that evening, the sun was setting over the city, creating a pale pink blanket across the sky, and he noticed that he felt wonderful!

When you are feeling sad or lonely, take a step outside of yourself and reach out to another person. It will help a great deal.

"Everybody can be great...because anybody can serve. You don't have to have a college degree to serve. You don't have to make your subject and verb agree to serve. You only need a heart full of grace. A soul generated by love."

—Martin Luther King, Jr.

Each of us in our own way, can put positive energy into making this a better world. Our small gestures create a ripple effect that spreads further than our imagination can possibly grasp.

"We can do no great things—only small things with great love."
—Mother Teresa

Do Your Little Bit of Good

"Happiness is not so much in having as in sharing. We make a living by what we get, but we make a life by what we give."
—Winston Churchill

When you think back on a beloved friend or family member, do you notice that it is their little acts of kindness that stick with you? Being aware of the power of small acts of thoughtfulness can help to guide you toward the kind of life you want to live.

We often think of gifts as material things. But the biggest gift is giving of ourselves. Around election time, especially during a very challenging election, a friend of mine e-mails and calls her neighbors and friends and asks them if they would like to join her at the polls. She offers to drive them there and have lunch with them. One of my neighbors shovels snow for the older folks in the neighborhood, free of charge. I know a couple who frequently walk in my neighborhood. When they see trash on our street, they pick it up. Little gestures of kindness go a long way for both the giver and the receiver.

A smile is such a simple thing to offer to the people you encounter in your daily life—waiters, grocery clerks, salespersons, neighbors, colleagues— and it is amazing how often it comes back to you. David Dunn, author of *Try Giving Yourself Away*, describes a smile as a sample of what you are in your heart. So when you smile you are sharing a part of your inner self with others.

"Do your little bit of good where you are; it's those little bits of good put together that overwhelm the world."
—Bishop Desmond Tutu

Spread Your Love

"Spread love everywhere you go; first of all in your own house. Give love to your children, to your wife or husband, to a next door neighbor...let no one ever come to you without leaving better and happier."

—**Mother Teresa**

In our very busy world, it is easy to become preoccupied with day-to-day activities and not be as considerate of others as we would wish to be. But by simply practicing the mindset of consideration, one can develop and expand it. After a while, it will become natural to you.

My friend Bill told the story of a neighbor of his who tended to behave distantly towards others but who had a very charming wife. When the couple moved out of the neighborhood, people began talking negatively about him. "He's a snob," said one. "He always seems tightly-wound!" griped another. A quiet young police officer in the group remained silent. Finally, someone asked him why he wasn't joining the criticism.

"I learned at the police academy not to form judgments until I had all of the facts," he replied. "I recently discovered from a colleague that the amiable wife of our disliked neighbor was an addicted gambler." He went on to explain how the perpetually stressed-out husband was continually trying to prevent his wife from gambling away all of their hard-earned money and resources.

"**Great Spirit, help me never to judge another until I have walked two weeks in his moccasins.**"

—**Sioux Indian Prayer**

"**Be kind whenever possible. It is always possible.**"

—**Dalai Lama**

Understanding Your Dreams

It can be very rewarding to develop an understanding of your dreams. We all have rich dream lives which are working in our favor.

"A dream is a theatre in which the dreamer himself is the scene, the player, the prompter, the producer, the author, the public and the critic."

—Carl Jung

Since the dawn of humanity, cultures around the world have consulted dreams for messages of guidance. Some describe dreams as an opportunity to eavesdrop on conversations between our conscious and our unconscious.

"The breeze at dawn has secrets to tell you. Don't go back to sleep."
—Jelaluddin Rumi

Here are some ways to gain a deeper understanding of your dream life:

- When you go to bed, tell yourself that you are interested in recalling your dreams.
- Keep a dream journal. Have a pen and pad at your bedside so that you can write down your dreams while they are still fresh in your mind.
- If you have a problem or concern about which you would like to gain clarity, before going to sleep ask for guidance in your dreams concerning that issue.
- If you want to improve your golf swing, piano playing, cooking, parenting technique or anything else, practice it in your mind before going to sleep. You may find that the practice is continuing on into your dreams.

Dream Interpretation

"Our dreams are most peculiarly independent of our consciousness and exceedingly valuable because they cannot cheat."

—Carl Jung

When you first wake up after having a dream, try to stay still in your bed until you have replayed the dream in your mind. Repeat the dream story to yourself (or another person) once again before getting up. Then write down the dream in your journal, in the present tense as if it were happening now. Include the emotions that you felt in the dream. For example: "I am on a bus. I look out of the window of the bus and see a small child waving to me. I am pleased."

During the day, take some time to reflect on the dream. Allow the images and sensations to come into your mind. Sink back into the dream experience. Let your dream evolve and do its work for you. Don't try to analyze it.

Tell your dream to someone again or read it out loud. You might find more details. If you do, add them to your journal description.

Now put all of this aside for a few days or weeks. Then, when you revisit your dream, reflect on how it relates to your life. Pay attention to the symbols and patterns. They have messages for you. If you have time, draw a picture of one or more of the symbols, add color, notice your thoughts and feelings and, if possible, give your dream a title.

Dreams are not time-bound like memories and reminiscences. You may have a dream that takes place in your childhood with aspects of your present life occurring in it at the same time.

"When read correctly, (dream) images tell us who we are instead of who we think we are."

—Montague Ullman

Affirmations

Affirmations can be very powerful tools for strengthening self-esteem. By thinking positive thoughts about yourself and practicing them daily, you are setting up your neural pathways to move in a positive direction.

Many people unconsciously say things to themselves regularly that trigger bad feelings, disappointments and sometimes depression. When you repeat regular affirmations, you are counteracting this negative self-talk. It is like the immune system. When it is built up, it fights diseases. Your psychological immune system can be strengthened by positive self-talk.

Here are some examples:

- I acknowledge and accept what I feel. I don't criticize myself.
- I am developing more confidence in myself—I believe in myself!
- I am learning how to tune into my body, appreciate and respect it.
- I am able to survive and I have the courage to heal myself.
- I am learning to appreciate my life, moment by moment.
- I am courageous.
- I have gifts to give in this world.
- I belong here.
- My friends love me and I love them.

Before drifting off to sleep at night, repeat your affirmations to yourself. This will help your subconscious to do its nighttime work for you and help to build powerfully positive neural networks.

Aging: Stay Positive

"Old age, believe me, is a good and pleasant thing. It is true you are gently shouldered off the stage, but then you are given such a comfortable front stall as a spectator."

—Confucius

There is so much negativity around the subject of aging that one forgets that it is simply part of life and has many good points! You can feel the earth closer to your feet now as you become more grounded and comfortable living in this world than you were as a young person. The potential is there for a deeper understanding of the self and others in ways that you might not have imagined when you were younger, because you now experience life through a broader lens.

The autumn leaves have brighter colors, sunrises spreading across cloud-filled purple skies are more vibrant, music is richer and more exciting and friendships are deeper. You are aware that your time here is short. After having experienced being alive for so long, you tend to develop a kind of knowing and awe that carries you through each day, despite some possible physical aches and pains of aging.

When reminiscing, you discover the potential for positive memories to grow more vivid in your recollections. There is also the opportunity to revisit some negative memories and explore ways that you can better understand them from this new vantage point.

"Age does not protect you from love. But love to some extent protects you from age.

—Anais Nin

Value your friendships. As you age, family begins to dwindle and close friends may know you at a deeper level than family members do. Stay connected with friends who are younger than you, too, and preferably the ones who have a positive outlook. Their spirit will help to keep you in a youthful frame of mind, while you will have the chance to provide mentorship for them.

"It is all that the young can do for the old, to shock them and keep them up to date."

—George Bernard Shaw

Keep dreaming and setting new goals. When you build plans for a future, there is more likely to be one!

Aging: Inner Ripening

"Inside every older person is a younger person wondering what happened."

—Jennifer Unlimited

As you age, pay close attention to your inner ripening. Get in the habit of tuning inward and becoming curious about your body, mind and spirit. This will help you to develop a gradual comfort and ease with your aging process.

"Know that you are the perfect age. Each year is special and precious, for you shall only live once. Be comfortable with growing older."

—Louise L. Hay

On some days, you might experience aches and pains more than on other days. During those achy periods, you may really feel "old." Attending an exercise or yoga class, going for a walk or a swim, or working on even a small project can help lift your spirits and improve your sense of self. It often takes a "self-push" to get started, but once you get going you'll soon feel like a new person.

"There are days of oldness, and then one gets young again. It goes backward and forward, not in one direction."

—Katharine Butler Hathaway

Aging: You're as Young as You Think

Age is just a number. It is possible feel physically and mentally younger than your "number." Dr. Ellen Langer, Professor of Psychology at Harvard University, conducted an intriguing research project on this subject. The research attempted to determine whether changing her subjects' mindset regarding their own age might lead to changes in their health and fitness.

Dr. Langer and her team of four graduate students gathered a group of volunteers who were male nursing home residents in their late seventies and early eighties. They took the group on a one-week retreat held in an isolated New England hotel. Participants were asked to live as though it were the year 1959. Newspapers, magazines, radio, TV programs and movies were dated from that year. "Current" events discussions were held and Elvis Presley and his contemporaries' music played. The men were asked not to reminisce about 1959 but to actually *live* the year during the retreat.

After only one week, the men showed physical signs of being younger. They had lower blood pressure, improved bone density, better hearing, higher quality memory, better dexterity, increased appetite, decreased arthritis symptoms, improved mental acuity and other indications of better health.

Never doubt that the way you think affects the way you feel! You can read more about this in *Counterclockwise* by Ellen Langer and learn how mental state can have profound effects on one's body.

"I think it is very encouraging to people who are actually 80 and think they are too old to do anything to know you can be stronger at 78 than

when you were at 30 or 40. I am more determined, and there's shorter time for me on Earth, I know that."

—Jane Goodall

"To find joy in work is to discover the fountain of youth."

—Pearl S. Buck

"Work" in this context refers to much more than paid employment. It can be any project or activity that you are passionate about.

Aging: Look Good, Feel Good

By making subtle shifts in your thinking and expectations, you can create significant improvements in your health and well-being.

A friend of mine was describing the owner of a bookstore to me. He described the woman as 74 years old, with blond curly hair and a cute figure. "I saw her as a 20-year-old with wrinkled skin!" he said.

You don't have to attempt to look 50 years younger than you are, but it can be helpful to put extra effort into your appearance and manner of dress. This can be uplifting and help you experience more involvement in the world, which in turn can boost your immune system and even add a few years to your life span. Just as how you think on the inside affects how you feel physically, your outer appearance affects how you feel emotionally.

"Live as if you were to die tomorrow. Learn as if you were to live forever."

—Gandhi

"The quality, not the longevity, of one's life is what is important."
—Martin Luther King, Jr.

Spiritual Growth

"Grow spiritually and help others to do so; it is the meaning of life."
—Leo Tolstoy

"We are not human beings having a spiritual experience. We are spiritual beings having a human experience."

—Ram Dass

The following mindful exercise will help you to make contact with your deeper self and spirit. Find a comfortable place to sit or lie down. Close your eyes and imagine that you are standing on the bank of a raging river. As you stand there, just watch the river instead of being in it. Now imagine that that river symbolizes your mind, thoughts and feelings. You are watching all of the action instead of it being a part of you. Now take a slow, deep, cleansing breath, and now another one. Sit in stillness for at least five or ten minutes. Give your body full permission to relax and let go. Then, when you are ready, open your eyes.

"People travel to wonder at the height of the mountains, at the huge waves of the seas, at the long course of the rivers, at the vast compass of the ocean, at the circular motion of the stars, and yet they pass by themselves without wondering."

—St. Augustine

"When you have only two pennies left in the world, buy a loaf of bread with one and a lily with the other."

—Chinese Proverb

Remember, each of us is a magnificent miracle and we are living in a wondrous world.

Deepening Your Appreciation for Life

"People usually consider walking on water or in thin air a miracle. But I think the real miracle is not to walk either on water or in thin air, but to walk on earth. Every day we are engaged in a miracle which we don't even recognize: a blue sky, white clouds, green leaves, the black, curious eyes of a child – our own two eyes. All is a miracle."

—Thich Nhat Hanh

Try this sometime: if you are feeling sad, lonely, low or just want to clear your head and enjoy the world, take a walk in a woodsy area, such as a park or local trail. Do this for about an hour. Then notice how you feel afterward. Chances are, things will look much better!

"The human venture depends absolutely on this quality of awe and reverence and joy in the Earth and all that lives and grows upon the Earth. As soon as we isolate ourselves from these currents of life, and from the profound mood that these engender within us, then our basic life satisfactions are diminished.

—Thomas Berry

When you take that walk in the woods, experiencing the beauty of the trees, the sky, birds, and the sensation of the earth beneath your feet, notice "the profound mood that these engender within us," in the words of Thomas Berry. Take these walks on a regular basis and notice how you touch your very own spirit and immerse yourself in the fullness of your life.

Spirituality and Life's Wonders

"The world will never starve for want of wonders, but for want of wonder."

—G. K. Chesterton

"If we could see the miracle of a single flower clearly, our whole life would change."

—Buddha

Do you ever go along wondering when your life is finally going to take a turn for the better when all of a sudden, everything seems to fall into place? Do you ever think about that shift as a miracle? Dr. Deepak Chopra describes this concept from the standpoint of Vedanta (Hindu philosophy).

As one moves toward a higher level of consciousness, two things tend to develop. First, the person stops worrying and becomes lighthearted and joyful. The second thing that happens is they encounter meaningful coincidences and synchronicities. As this process accelerates, one starts experiencing the miraculous.

Deepak Chopra has written many books on spirituality. A very popular one is *Seven Spiritual Laws of Success.*

Death and Dying

In *Staring at the Sun*, psychiatrist Irvin Yalom describes how deep connections with others help to soften the fear of death. He reminds us that we were not here before we were born, and that our time here is very brief.

In *Final Gifts, Understanding the Special Awareness, Needs and Communications of the Dying*, co-authors and hospice nurses Maggie Callahan and Patricia Kelley provide numerous first-person stories about those who are dying and the people who care about them. They often found that when a person is nearing death, they see someone who is invisible to others who serves as a guide to assist them through the transition from life into death. Because of the hundreds of stories that Callahan and Kelley have heard from their patients, they believe that people don't actually die alone and that some spiritual beings will be companions on the journey.

"Dying is easy, it's living that scares me to death."
—Annie Lennox

"I had seen birth and death but had thought they were different."
—T.S. Eliot

"When it's over, I want to say all my life I was a bride married to amazement. I was a bridegroom, taking the world into my arms."
—Mary Oliver

Rewriting Your Scripts

Sometimes it can be helpful to revisit old issues that caused you problems as a way of re-processing them, helping you to move forward and feel more safety in the present. When memories remain unprocessed, they are stored in the brain in such a way that the related emotions and physical sensations are stuck. By revisiting these memories in a calmer state of mind, you have an opportunity to release the associated feelings from their stuck position.

Here is an exercise that can help you to better understand and process these issues from your past. Take some slow, deep breaths and allow your body to relax. Now go back in time to a memory of an unsafe situation that caused you some problems, but wasn't a major trauma. Take some more slow, deep breaths. As you think of that memory in a relaxed state, you may find that your hearing is expanded and you are able hear more from that memory than you'd heard in past versions of it. For some people, memories are more visual and you might find that you are able to see aspects of the problem situation that you couldn't see in the past. This could prove to be very helpful to you in gaining new perspectives on old issues. However, if you find that doing this exercise causes you too much discomfort, it is best to arrange to work with a therapist on these issues.

Another exercise to help resolve a negative memory is "wishful rewriting" of your story. Close your eyes, go inside, and take a slow deep breath and help yourself to relax. Now, think of the unpleasant memory, but this time rewrite the script in your mind and change the story with a more satisfying resolved ending. Now open your eyes and write the new story on paper. This technique works very well with unsettling dreams, too. When you rewrite your script, you'll experience a sense of empowerment.

The Power of Our Thoughts

"Our best friends and our worst enemies are our thoughts. A thought can do us more good than a doctor or a banker or a faithful friend. It can also do us more harm than a brick."

—Dr. Frank Crane

When things get off track, we often tell ourselves all kinds of negative things that can limit our freedom of action and actually cement our negative behavior rather than help us to change it. "This is a disaster!" "I'm so stupid!" Such words can make us feel worse than we already are, and cause a swift downward spiral.

Your thoughts control your life. What you think about often happens. When a difficult situation occurs and you become overwhelmed, tell yourself that it all will work out well. Take a deep breath, remind yourself that you are safe, and again tell yourself that all will be well. Repeat it over and over again like a chant. This will soothe you.

You might not have control over everything that you do, but you *do* have control over how you think about those things. Some people are not even aware that they are having negative thoughts. Get in the habit of noticing your thinking. It will put you in a good position to make the necessary changes to create a better life.

"The only thing we are ever dealing with is a thought, and a thought can be changed."

—Louise L. Hay

The Three A's

The Three A's were developed through the ALANON program. They provide a simple and effective technique for learning how to live honestly with yourself and help you realize that you have choices.

First, become **AWARE** of the reality of your situation. This may be harder than it sounds because you might think of what you *should* feel but not what you really feel. You might be very uncomfortable with your situation but not want to face reality. For example, let's say that you are unhappy with your living situation. Awareness opens your eyes to squarely face your feelings about it.

The next step is **ACCEPTANCE.** Think of acceptance not as a form of resignation, but as a way of noticing what is happening. You accept the fact that you are unhappy with your living situation. Acceptance helps you to become aware of being in charge of your own life and making your own choices. You are accepting the reality of what is happening to you in the moment.

Step three is **ACTION.** For example, you may take action to explore new options for places to live that will help you out of the negative living environment. Any small action can interrupt inertia, be empowering, and bring you closer to a resolution that can provide hope. Simply making a telephone call can energize you and move you closer to the goal.

It helps to go through this process for several rounds as follows:

I accept that—-
I am aware that—-
My action is to—

"If you don't like the scene you're in, if you're unhappy, if you're lonely, change your scene. Paint a new backdrop."

Leo Buscaglia

Know What You Really Want

In *Alice in Wonderland*, Alice asks the Cheshire Cat where to go. "It depends on where you want to go," the cat replies. "I don't much care," says Alice. "Then it doesn't matter which way you go," concludes the cat.

The clearer you are about your goals, the better chance you have of reaching them. This may sound like pure common sense, but you'd be surprised how many people haven't thought clearly about what they really want!

Sometimes, WPT (What People Think) gets in the way. Of course it is important to think about how others see you, but you need to strike a healthy balance. You want to be considerate of others but also live an authentic life. When it is all over, you don't want other people's names engraved on your tombstone!

Take responsibility for your own life in everything that you do. Don't blame others for your problems and mistakes. We all confront problems and make mistakes; the key is to learn and grow from them. Get in the habit of thinking positively. Build on your positive actions and they will grow.

"It is only by following your deepest instinct that you can lead a rich life."

—Katharine Butler Hathaway

Find the Courage to Move Ahead

"We have a need to know where we stand and how we stand. It's a sense of having a stable core, a center of gravity that allows us to feel we claim our spot on the planet and claim our membership in the human race."

—Belleruth Naparstack

After the devastating earthquakes in Haiti in 2009, some of the women who were living in makeshift tents braided each others' hair, put on makeup and stood tall in order to feel like things were normal and under control. The women performed these rituals regularly in order to give each other hope.

"The only courage that matters is the kind that gets you from one moment to the next."

—Mignon McLaughlin

Virginia Satir said that the main message she wanted to be remembered for was that "the event does not determine the behavior." She believed that our thoughts about the events were what counted.

"You gain strength, courage and confidence by every experience by which you really stop to look fear in the face. You are able to say to yourself: "I lived through this horror. I can take the next thing that comes along."

—Eleanor Roosevelt

Understanding Anger

Anger is a natural emotion. Consider it a signal that something isn't right. Notice how it feels in your body, but don't let it rule you. Instead, think of your anger as an opportunity for change. It is important to understand your anger so that you can process it, do something to change the circumstances and then let it go. Holding on to anger can be very harmful to you.

"Anger is an acid which can do more harm to the vessel in which it is stored, than anything into which it is poured."
—Mark Twain

Your "old brain," also known as the reptilian brain, kicks into fight-or-flight mode when you feel threatened. It exists to ensure your safety and survival. When activated, it quickens the breathing and releases adrenaline. Sometimes it can push you into a blame- game state where you insist: "I'm right and you're wrong!" At such times you want to be able to access the logical part of your brain in order to calm down. But as the saying goes, "When the blood pressure goes up the I.Q. goes down!" In other words, from a physical standpoint the thinking brain is hard to reach during times of high stress. It is in a sleeping state in order to make room to fight, flight or freeze.

The best thing to do at these times is to pause and take time out to disengage from the grip of anger. This will calm down your mind and body and give you a chance to engage the logical part of your brain so that you can make rational decisions.

Here is where counting to ten and taking a deep breath can really help! Other tranquility-promoting activities include taking a walk, doing some brief meditation, praying, reading your list of gratitudes or journaling to sort out troubling issues. After a while, you will have calmed down and the logical part of your brain will kick in again.

$\mathcal{D}$ealing with $\mathcal{A}$nger

Stop, Breathe, Think and Act. Stop, take a deep breath and count to ten. Press the pause button. Prevent runaway angry feelings from taking over.

I am in line at the grocery store with a full cart and a time schedule to meet. A woman steps in front of me. I stop and notice anger welling up in my body. I feel flushed and my heart is racing. I feel like I am being treated unfairly and ignored. I take a deep breath, count to ten, and instead of talking right away I think about what I need to do. In this case I say to the woman: "Excuse me, I think I was in front of you." If she apologizes and steps back, the problem is resolved. If she becomes nasty, I have to take another breathe, count to ten again, and consider a second plan of action, which in this case might be to ask to speak to the store manager.

You will receive many invitations to get angry. A co-worker makes an abrupt, inappropriate comment in your direction, your teenager is rude to you, your spouse has a bad day and attempts to take it out on you, or the cat has a bad night and you are her target. Often, you find yourself unprepared for these situations. Stay mindful of the importance of stopping, taking a deep breath counting to ten, going inside to figure out how to handle the situation, taking care of yourself and also remaining respectful of the other person.

Be aware that you have *choices*. Feeling anger is normal, but it's what you do with it that counts. Use anger as a cue. When you are thirsty, that is a cue to take a drink of water. When you are angry, that is a cue to take a deep breath, pause and figure out how to handle the situation appropriately.

There are numerous extremely helpful books on dealing with anger including the following: *The Dance of Anger*, by Harriet Lerner, Ph.D., *Anger: Wisdom for Cooling the Flames*, by Thich Nhat Hahn and *When Anger Hurts: Quieting the Storm Within*, by Matthew McKay, Peter D. Rogers and Judith McKay.

The Power of Compromise

Do not teach your children never to be angry. Teach them how to be angry."

—Lyman Abbott

Sometimes, you find yourself in an argument with a friend or family member that feels like it is getting out of hand. At that point, tell the other person that you need to leave and will come back when you calm down. Give them an approximate time, such as fifteen minutes, but if you think that you need one or two hours, don't hesitate to tell them. Ask them not to follow you when you leave.

It helps to understand that there are degrees of anger and related emotions. There is mild irritation, disappointment, hurt, frustration, and so on. The more aware you are of these feelings, the more you can notice when they are starting to get intense. Acknowledge your feelings to yourself. Don't ignore them.

Listen to the other person's point of view in a way that shows respect for both yourself and for them. Set up a time and place to have your discussion with no interruptions. Allow plenty of time to work through the problems. Avoid making accusations and finger pointing (blaming). Don't use words such as "always" and "never," as in "You are always late" or "You never support me."

Be willing to compromise and stay focused on the behavior that you are seeking. For example: "I would like for us to explore ways that we can both be on time for our commitments." Being very specific in these situations will help a great deal.

"It is never what people do that makes us angry; it's what we tell ourselves about what they did that makes us angry."

—Marshall Rosenberg

Strengthening Your Self-Esteem

Dr. Wendy Schain, a psychologist who counsels people who have cancer, describes self-esteem as a set of four bank accounts:

1. The net worth of your **Physical Self,** which consists of your physical appearance and the health and well-being of your body.
2. Your **Social Self,** which is your emotional support system consisting of friends, family, co-workers, and others who care about you.
3. Your **Achieving Self,** which relates to what you have accomplished at work, school, and in important relationships.
4. Your **Spiritual Self,** which represents your religious and moral beliefs and the strength that they provide you.

In the course of a lifetime, deposits are made in each of these accounts. But when a crisis occurs, you find that you have to make withdrawals from one or more of the accounts. For example, if you develop a serious illness, going through treatment may be expensive, take a lot of time and reduce some of your physical capacity to function. It can also cause problems with relationships and career goals and even at times your faith in God. When "funds" from any one of the above-mentioned accounts become low, you may find that you need to take out a loan from one of the others in order to balance your account.

During these times, it makes a lot of sense to put effort into making new deposits in the accounts that remain active. By doing this, you'll find that a withdrawal in one area of your self-esteem will not put you in bankruptcy. For example, if your medical condition has affected your appearance, you might wish to focus on the love and care you receive from friends and family who relate to you in a positive and intimate way.

Dr. Schain's bank account system is an excellent way to see your life as a many-faceted whole and figure out which areas are in need of replenishment.

Self-Esteem: Be Your Own Support System

It is important to be aware of you own needs as well as those of others. Know that you deserve to feel good and help yourself to become aware of what gives you comfort. There are times when you need support and no one is available to provide it for you. At those times, you need to know how to provide that support for yourself.

Be aware of the language of choice. For example:

- "I've decided…"
- "I am choosing…"
- "I am willing…"
- "I am not willing…"

Self-esteem is always there, but it can vary in strength from moment to moment. Sometimes we feel very confident and competent, while other times we might find ourselves feeling low.

Virginia Satir grew up on a farm in Wisconsin. On her family's back porch was a huge black iron pot, which had lovely rounded sides and stood on three legs. Virginia's mother made her own soap, so for part of the year the pot was filled with soap.

When threshing crews came through in the summer, her mother filled the pot with stew. At other times of the year her father used the pot to store manure for her mother's flower beds. The family eventually called the pot the "3-S pot." Anyone who wanted to use the pot had to ask two questions: "What is in the pot now and how full is it?"

As human beings, we might feel full, empty, dirty and sometimes even cracked. Think about your individual pot and notice what you are feeling in it now. Are there feelings of worth; are you at peace, or are you holding some anger or self-criticism? Get in the habit of checking in with yourself regularly. Take time to sort out your feelings and then express your needs. This will put you on the path to strong self-esteem.

"The turning point in the process of growing up is when you discover the core strength within you that survives all hurt."

—Max Lerner

Fully Living the Journey

Get in the habit of being ready for life. There is a Zen saying: "When the student is ready, the teacher will appear." Opportunities are all around us, but often we are not aware of them. Teachers and mentors are standing by, waiting for us to notice them and seek their guidance.

"We shall not cease from explorations, and the end of all our explorations will be to arrive where we started and know the place for the first time."

—T.S. Eliot

As you continue your journey, consider the following:

Studies show that when you share, volunteer and give to charity, reward regions of the brain light up. Some of the data suggests that you will have a longer lifespan if you think from a generous perspective. It is important for you to honor your altruistic nature. To read more about this fascinating subject see Dr. Dacher Keltner's book: *Born to be Good: The Science of a Meaningful Life.*

"Act as if what you do makes a difference. It does."

—William James

"You may not have saved a lot of money in your life, but if you have saved a lot of heartaches for other folks, you are a pretty rich man."

—Seth Parker

People underestimate the power of positive physical touch. We all need to touch and be touched. As human beings, touch was the first language we learned. It affects our emotions and perception of the world. Even small touches—a supportive touch on the arm or back by a teacher, a sympathetic touch from a doctor or a hand shake from a coach can have a powerful impact. Couples who tend to touch each other often, report more satisfaction.

"There is more hunger for love and appreciation in this world than for bread."

—**Mother Teresa**

Mother Teresa believed deeply in the power of loving physical touch.

Be Assertive

You will not be liked by everyone. The important thing is to respect yourself and others. Being assertive means that you stand up for your rights in such a way that the rights of others are not violated. In other words, you say what you feel in an appropriate way, without hurting others.

Many people find it hard to say "no." But sometimes, saying "no" helps you to keep your balance. If you wait too long to set boundaries with other people, you will feel anger or resentment rising in your body. This may manifest itself as tightness in your chest, shallow breathing, queasy stomach or rubbery legs. Your body is providing vital information to you. Learn how to read the messages. They will serve you well!

You might be extending yourself further than you really want to. Check inside of yourself and notice what is a true "yes" and a true "no" for you in this and in every situation. As you discover what really fits for you, you and will get closer to your true nature.

With time and practice, you will learn how to distinguish between healthy relationships and ones that make you feel drained. You will be able to say "no" or "yes" with more confidence and develop a sense peace within yourself.

When you become aware that you really do have choices, you will experience a deep sense of freedom. You will not lose your friends and family if you occasionally say "no."

A favorite book of mine on assertiveness is: *Your Perfect Right: A Guide to Assertive Behavior*, by Robert Alberti, Ph.D. and Michael Emmons, Ph.D.

Practicing Relaxation

You may be carrying around extra anxiety and not be aware of it. In order to help yourself relax try this: close your eyes, take a deep breath and check inside. Notice what your body is doing. If you experience any tight places, give each tight place a message of appreciation for letting you know that it is there. Then give yourself permission to relax and take another slow, deep cleansing breath.

If you you are flooded with anxiety, go to a part of your body that is calm. For example, you might not have any discomfort in your right big toe! In you mind, go to that toe, and be in touch with what it feels like. If it is a calm sensation, let that calmness spread through your body. Now take another deep breath. This is a simple but very helpful relaxation technique.

Repeat this message to yourself slowly three times: "Be as you are." Now take one more slow, deep breath.

For further information on relaxation practices read Dr. Joan Borysenko's *Inner Peace for Busy People: 52 simple Strategies for Transforming Your Life.*

Setting Up Order in Your Life

When your physical world is in order, your mental world will feel more peaceful. Make a regular habit of keeping your home in order and decorating it in a pleasing manner. After all, this is what you will be looking at every day! Set up plants, hang pictures on the walls, paint the rooms with colors that you love and surround yourself with beauty. You don't have to spend a lot of money to make this happen. Discount stores, yard sales and consignment shops can offer many attractive things for you to choose from.

Spend a few minutes a day putting things away so that your rooms are neat and clean. Don't let mail, clothes, and unwashed dishes accumulate from the day before. Remember, it only takes a few minutes to hang up a coat and rinse off a few dishes. By doing this, you will look forward to coming home each day! If you find that things get way out of hand, enlist a friend or relative to help you get order back in your home.

Build and enrich a support system of friends, co-workers and family members. Take breaks at work and at home and just relax. In this busy world, people who are entitled to lunch and midday breaks often eat at their desks. This is a bad habit. It helps to get out, go for a walk and eat lunch outside of your office. The important thing is to get away for a while. If you have an enclosed office, you might want to occasionally close the door and put your feet up. Give your mind and body a real break and a chance to unwind and relax even for just five or ten minutes.

When it comes to problems, be proactive. If you notice a minor problem developing, deal with it before it becomes a major headache. In the long run, this approach will save you a lot of grief. Four very dangerous words are: "It will go away." For example, if your roof is leaking, you might put down pots to collect the water for a little while. But pretty soon, you have to face the fact that you will need to repair or replace the roof—or get thoroughly soaked!

Prioritize and Enrich Your Life

Put first things first. If you have something that needs to be attended to right away, get right to it and don't waste time on things that are less important. The more you get in the habit of doing this, the easier it will become because you will be developing new neural pathways and habits for **TCB** (Taking Care of Business).

Make a list of things that are troubling you. Then, next to each problem, write down what you intend to do about it. This worry list will help you to get things off your chest and out in the open so that you can realistically do your planning and problem-solving. It will also help you to sleep better at night because once your problems are on paper and you are analyzing how to resolve them, you have taken the first step towards putting you mind at rest.

As much as possible, be an assertive communicator. Avoid finger-pointing and blaming others. No one wins in the blame game.

Reward yourself when you do something well. Appreciate your good days and remember them when you have a bad one. Pat yourself on the back—literally—when you do something that you are proud about.

Take up a hobby or two that you can enjoy on a regular basis. Set aside time each day just to think about your life, your plans and dreams. Eat a balanced diet and do some exercise each day. If you drink alcoholic or sugary beverages, do so in moderation. Avoid smoking. Keep in touch with friends. Embrace your life!

Cut Back on Worries

When possible, try to be flexible. Know that things are changing around you all the time. The better you can adapt to change and enjoy it, the happier you will be.

"It is not the strongest of the species that survives, nor the most intelligent that survives. It is the one that is the most adaptable to change."

—Charles Darwin

Don't waste your time with worries. They will not solve problems. When my mother was in her late eighties, she told me that she had only one regret: "I wish I hadn't worried so much." In older age, she discovered that ninety percent of the things she worried about never came to pass and she found a way to deal with the ones that did transpire.

"Today is the tomorrow we worried about yesterday."

—Mark Twain

Relaxation Techniques

I'm going to show you a very quick, simple and powerful stress management technique. As you do it, it's helpful to inhale through your nose and exhale through your mouth. I realize that this is not always possible for everyone because of sinus or other problems. If that is the case for you, breathing in and out through your mouth is fine, too.

Sit in a comfortable chair, close your eyes and take three slow, deep breaths. Select a color in your mind that is soothing to you. Mentally immerse yourself in that color. Take three more slow, deep breaths.

Now select a soothing sound that seems to fit with the color. Take three additional slow, deep breaths.

Next, notice any body sensations that you're having as you imagine the color and the sound. By the term "body sensations" I mean any physical feelings that you are aware of at this time. Take three more slow, deep breaths. Now, gently open your eyes and notice how your feel. Many people find that this exercise helps them to relax in a very short period of time. It takes only about five minutes!

Another brief stress management exercise:

Lie on your back on a bed or exercise mat. Place one hand on your abdomen, near your navel. Inhale through you nose and exhale through your mouth three times. Become aware that your hand is rising and falling on your stomach with each breath.

For a few minutes, concentrate on slow, even breathing. This is a good exercise to do as you are getting ready to go to sleep. It is also very helpful when you are under stress and simply want to relax your body-mind.

Managing Stress at Work

If you find that your workdays are filled with stressful minutes, it's important to become aware of what is going on and how to get yourself back in balance so that those minutes don't turn into hours. Do some journaling to figure out where the stressors are and what you need to do to change the situation. Sometimes it is a matter of making some small adjustments.

"The art of being wise is the art of knowing what to overlook."
—William James

Be aware of your physical symptoms. Your body won't lie to you, so pay attention to it. Many aches and pains are stress-related.

Most people don't enjoy doing paperwork but once you do it, it's done. Be aware of how great you feel when you tie up those loose ends. With larger projects, try doing a little each day.

Build a supportive relationship with your boss. By understanding her pressures, and connecting with her, you will find respectful ground between you. With this kind of relationship, you can more easily get her to respect you and understand your needs.

When you are working on a project, keep interruptions to a minimum. It might be necessary to close your door for a short while or put up a sign requesting that you not be disturbed. Set up periods of time when it is okay to be interrupted, but the rest of the time stay focused on your work.

Managing Stress at Home

"Perhaps the greatest social service that can be rendered by anybody to the country and to mankind is to bring up a family."
—George Bernard Shaw

Shaw was certainly right about that, but bringing up a family can be very stressful! When possible, try to spread out major events over periods of time. For example, for many parents September is an extremely busy month with summer ending and school starting up. By keeping their calendar as free as possible from other commitments during that month, many parents find it easier to manage the busy times.

Work towards being at peace with your family and friends. Use humor—remember that laughter releases vital biochemicals within the body and helps to break up the tensions that build up in the family from time to time. Find a way to improve your home life every day in one small way.

Learn how to live in the moment. Tune in to yourself and say: "How can I take care of myself in a better way—*right now?*" For example, ask your spouse to watch the children for a short while so that you can take a nap or go for a walk. Schedule regular time to get to the gym, have lunch with a friend or go shopping. Ask family members to help out with meal preparation and clean-up. Even amid family responsibilities, take the time to care for yourself. The more you care for yourself, the more energy and joy you will have available. You will then be in a much better position to reach out to other family members.

Think of self-care as respecting your mind, body and spirit. See yourself as a tree with beautiful long branches. If you were to cut off each branch and give it away, saving none for yourself, you would be left with just a stump. So it is important to preserve some of the rich, nourishing branches for yourself.

Be a planner. Failing to plan is planning to fail. The clearer your plans are, the more likely you will be to carry them out in a way that will help you and your family to feel good. For example, if you want to set up a family vacation, sit down with your family, calendar in hand, and discuss dates and destinations with everybody. Planning is what makes life happen!

Don't try to always prove yourself to be right. It is okay to admit that you made a mistake. Apologies help heal relationships.

Self Care

"One of the most courageous things you can do is identify yourself, know who you are, what you believe in, and where you want to go."
—Sheila Murray Bethel

When someone makes a request of you, it is okay to say: "Let me think about that and get back to you," rather than responding with an immediate "yes" or "no." Give yourself time to decide if the request really fits for you. (Of course, if that person happens to be your boss, you might have to say: "How soon do you need it?")

Keep an open mind about others. Wear your detective hat when you go out in the world and leave your judge's hat at home on the shelf in a closet.

Look for the positives in others.

Face and accept your human limitations. It is easy to see the faults in others but hard to see our own.

Remember, we don't achieve happiness when we pursue it as a specific goal. Instead, think about happiness as a byproduct, a result of your activities.

Avoid focusing on the past—especially regrets. It is a waste of time.

Take extra special care of yourself during times of grieving. Your mind, body and spirit will need a lot of time to heal. If possible, take time off from work so that you can process your loss. Make a special effort to stay connected to loved ones.

Self-Understanding

Set aside some "alone time" each day. If your busy schedule absolutely doesn't allow for this, plan to do it at least one day a week. Search deep inside yourself during those times of solitude to learn what is really important to you, and then go about working towards those goals. The better you understand yourself, the closer you will come to accomplishing what is most important to you.

"I see only one rule: to be clear. If I am not clear then my entire world crumbles into nothing."

—Marie Henri Beyle

Give yourself permission to let go of some things in order to make time for yourself. Remember, you can't do it all!

Simplify your life as much as possible. Set up brief de-cluttering periods now and then to give away, throw away or reorganize your personal belongings, so that they don't build up too much. Set aside time to check you calendar so that it doesn't get cluttered up, either. Learn to distinguish the difference between unimportant and important tasks.

Set up a long-range calendar so that you can see the big picture and how things fit together for you. Do this in pencil so that you can make necessary adjustments. It is also important to keep calendars so that activities are recorded on a regular basis. This keeps you focused on good time management.

At the end of your day, take a few minutes to reflect on how it went, and then plan for the next day so that you know what lies ahead. The fewer surprises, the better!

Physical Fitness

"My grandmother started walking five miles a day when she was sixty. She's ninety-five now, and we don't know where the hell she is."
—Ellen DeGeneres

We underestimate the value of exercise. Going on a 15 minute walk can completely change your frame of mind. Research has demonstrated that engaging in an enjoyable physical activity such as gardening, walking, dancing, swimming or yoga, will recharge your "happiness batteries" and put you in a good frame of mind. See the work of Shawn Achor in *The Happiness Advantage* for more information on the relationship between happiness, health and exercise.

One winter night many years ago, my sons, ages 8 and 10 at the time, got embroiled in a big argument. Before long, my husband got into it along with them. The house felt like a big noise box, and I could feel my body getting very tense. Suddenly I realized that I was getting upset about something that I had no control over! I checked with my husband to be sure that he had control of the situation and when he assured me that he did, I made a decision. I packed up my gym bag with a bathing suit and towel, and off I went to the pool!

I swam as many laps as I could, took a shower, and came home feeling wonderful. As I walked in the door I noticed that the three of them were still going at it. But my frame of mind had totally changed because I felt so good physically, mentally and emotionally. I looked at my husband and sons and thought about how lucky I was to have them in my life.

The Mind-Body Connection

Harvard psychology professor and researcher Dr. Ellen Langer conducted a study with hotel chambermaids to help them reframe their understanding of exercise. She explained to them that the Surgeon General considered that the exercise they got on their jobs met the qualifications of "real exercise." In other words, dusting, emptying trash, changing beds, cleaning bathrooms, vacuuming floors and other chores that they did on a daily basis were recognized as valuable as the exercise that a person would do in a gym or health club.

After they received this information, the chambermaids focused more on what they were doing on the job. In time, they lost weight, their physical markers changed and their blood pressure went down. Dr. Langer's book, *Counterclockwise*, describes this and related studies that demonstrate the power of the mind/body connection. Whatever you put in your mind, your body will experience.

When you are exercising, think about how you are taking good care of yourself. When you are physically fit you have more energy and you are guarding against ailments such as heart disease and cancer. As a bonus, regular exercise keeps us in a more positive frame of mind. So, you can't go wrong!

$\mathcal{F}$riendships

Maintaining positive connections with others is crucial to good mental, physical and spiritual health. Our friends help us know ourselves. Ram Dass puts this well when he says, "Only that in you which is in me can hear what I am saying."

Take time out once in a while to write a letter to a friend, stamp it and put it in a mailbox! People are so often texting, e-mailing or communicating on social networks. It is refreshing to receive a paper letter or thank-you note which expresses a kind of special care and concern.

Friends help to fulfill our lives. The ones that have stood the test of time and change help us to hold our history, as we help to hold theirs. It is healthy and enjoyable to make some new friends as well as continuing to cultivate the old ones. Friends energize us and help us to gain perspective, and they provide an opportunity for us to share joys and disappointments.

"It takes a long time to grow an old friend."

—John Leonard

Making New Friends

Most friendships start out superficially, but if you hang in there, many of them have the potential to become deeper over the years. It takes patience. It is good to have friends of varying ages and interests. Some friends may be "walking" or "fishing" friends, while others might be "movie," "coffee," "work" or "travel" friends. Still others might be "friends for life."

"Nobody sees a flower—really. It is so small. We haven't time, and to see takes time—like to have a friend takes time."

—Georgia O'Keeffe

As you age, you may find that your friends play an even larger role in your life than your family because of a variety of circumstances such as geographical location and lifestyle. Peers have a good understanding of you and your life and might sometimes understand you better than family members. Places to meet new friends include classes, volunteer programs, churches, book clubs, the workplace, and activity groups such as hiking clubs, tennis programs and ski clubs. If you are looking to meet new friends, keep an open mind and a welcoming smile on your face. Take an interest in others; ask them about themselves. The best way to make a friend is to be one.

Forgiveness

When you think about forgiveness, you might imagine that you are giving the other person a break or a gift. What you might not realize is that when you forgive another, you are unburdening yourself! In some situations, you actually might want to forgive in your heart and mind but not tell the other person about it. This may be the case when there is someone with whom you don't want to continue in any kind of relationship, but you do want to experience the forgiveness flowing within yourself. Forgiveness is a kind of letting go and releasing of pain.

"The man who cannot forgive destroys a bridge which he will have to cross, because every person needs forgiveness."
—Edward Herbert

"Without forgiveness life is governed by an endless cycle of resentment and retaliation."
—Robert Assagioli

As you search deep within your heart for forgiveness, you'll find yourself feeling much lighter. Holding on to those grudges only weighs you down and adds bitterness to your body and spirit.

Solitude

Everyone needs time alone to regroup, connect with themselves and to do internal work. At these times it is good to journal, go for a walk in the woods, take a hot bath, read a book, listen to music or engage in any number of other enjoyable, rejuvenating activities. You might want to practice a musical instrument, cook or just sit back and reflect on your life. We regenerate our batteries with solitude.

Sarah Ban Breathnach, author of *Simple Abundance: A Daybook of Comfort and Joy*, recommends that you spend time alone in order to "nurture your vision." It is very important to have a deep connection with yourself so that you can actually develop that vision. There is a relationship between the amount of stress one feels and the amount of time set aside for oneself daily.

"Being solitary is being luxuriously immersed in doing things of your own choice, aware of the fullness of your own presence."

—Ann Koller

"Women need solitude in order to find again the true essence of themselves."

—Anne Morrow Lindbergh

Men need solitude, too! Take small breaks every day and carve out time for longer ones when possible. Make it a top priority.

Gaining Perspective

Each person's life is totally unique, but each person's life is also very similar to that of others. Those who have been here before us have gone through many of the same situations, issues, joys, problems and accomplishments. Think about how you will feel about the current "problem du jour" ten years from now; five years from now. It takes on a different quality.

"At any given moment, life is completely senseless. But viewed over a period it seems to reveal itself as an organism existing in time, having a purpose, trending in a certain direction."

—Aldous Huxley

It is important to realize that while everyone is trying to accomplish big things, life is truly made up of many small things. Think about how you want to spend your time because that is how you will spend your life!

"Twenty years from now you will be more disappointed by the things you didn't do than the ones you did."

—Mark Twain

Our lives depend on the works of others who have come before us—both those who are alive and those who are no longer here. When you view your life with a wider lens, you perceive the things your're now doing that add to the world as well as the things that will remain after you leave this world.

"The true meaning of life is to plant trees, under whose shade you do not expect to sit."

—Nelson Henderson

"I long to accomplish great and noble tasks, but it is my chief duty to accomplish humble tasks as though they were great and noble. The world is moved along, not only by the mighty shoves of its heroes, but also but by the tiny pushes of each honest worker."

—Helen Keller

Keeping an Open Mind

There is an old story about a Chinese farmer and a horse that has been retold in many forms. It is a useful way to think about gaining perspective on your life.

As the story goes, the farmer has a horse and when his neighbor comes to visit he says: "Oh, how lucky you are to have a horse!" The farmer replies: "We'll see."

The very next day the farmer's horse runs away. When the neighbor comes over he is very sympathetic and says: "Oh, how unlucky you are that you lost your horse!" To that, the farmer replies: "We'll see."

A few days later the horse returns to his owner bringing with him a new mare. Before you know it, his neighbor is congratulating him on his good fortune but the farmer just says: "We'll see."

The next day, the farmer's son is riding the mare to break it in and the mare throws him on to the ground, breaking his leg. As you already know, the neighbor is once again very sympathetic.

In the last part of the story, the army comes to their village and is recruiting soldiers, but because the farmer's son has a broken leg, he is spared from the draft. When the neighbor says: "Oh how fortunate! Your son doesn't have to go in the army." The farmer just replies, once again: "We'll see."

This story is based on Taoism (pronounced Daoism), which emphasizes peace, detachment, receptiveness, naturalness and effortless action. Allowing life to unfold and keeping an open mind and a clear perspective will be immensely helpful to you. Problems that seem difficult at one moment can become opportunities in the future.

Characters in the Chinese language often have several meanings. The one for "crisis" is also "danger" and "opportunity."

DAY 99

Self-Discipline

At times, life can be quite difficult. As my friend Sgt. Finger used to say, "Life is just one problem after another." The key to it all, he believed, was to deal with each problem head-on, one at a time, and learn how to be an expert problem-solver.

At times being self-disciplined means delaying gratification. You have to be careful not to exchange what you want most in your future for what you might be craving at this particular moment.

"If we don't discipline ourselves, the world will do it for us."
—William Feather

"Some people regard discipline as a chore. For me it's a kind of order that sets me free to fly."
—Julie Andrews

"Mastering others is strength, mastering yourself is power."
—Lao Tzu

Be persistent and energetic. This will help you to build a strong sense of control over your own life. This, in turn, will contribute to a sense of peace.

I once heard someone say that talent without discipline was like an octopus on roller skates. You see plenty of movement, but no one ever knows if it is going to be forward, backwards or sideways. Discipline really makes all the difference.

If you would like to have a deeper understanding of the art of self-discipline, read *The Road Less Traveled,* by M. Scott Peck, M.D.

Patience

Patience with others is extremely important in life. Patience with yourself is at the heart of everything. So many situations in life require patience. We want to see it all happen quickly, get the answers right away, get over the pain now, solve our problems yesterday. But life doesn't work like that. As we cultivate patience, we become synchronized with life.

"A man who is a master of patience is a master of everything else."
—George Savile

"Adopt the pace of nature: her secret pace is patience."
—Ralph Waldo Emerson

If you ever do gardening, the above quote will make a lot of sense to you. When you plant seeds in the ground, you know that they will grow at their own pace. You cannot make them grow any faster than they are meant to grow, just as you know that you cannot push the river.

"I have just three things to teach: simplicity, patience, compassion. These three are your greatest treasures."

—Lao Tzu

Peace

"If there is light in the soul,
There will be beauty in the person.
If there is beauty in the person,
There will be harmony in the house.
If there is harmony in the house,
There will be order in the nation.
If there is order in the nation,
There will be peace in the world."

Chinese Proverb

Keep light in your soul and peace in your heart!